Super Sub

by Lorilynn

illustrated by Rex Schneider

cover by Margo DePaulis

Publisher
Instructional Fair • TS Denison
Grand Rapids, Michigan 49544

ISBN: 1-56822-959-3
Super Sub
Copyright © 2000 by Instructional Fair Group
a Tribune Education Company
3195 Wilson Dr. NW
Grand Rapids, Michigan 49544

Table of Contents

Chapter Four

Chapter Five

Chapter Six

Introduction

Being a substitute teacher is a demanding and often challenging task. It requires quick thinking, adaptability, and readiness for a variety of situations. The many unknown variables at play in a given classroom can be an equation for chaos if one does not enter prepared and confident.

While most teachers endeavor to leave clear, structured lesson plans when they must be away, there are times when this is not possible. In such cases, the substitute is left with little or no guidance and must rely on his/her own ingenuity. Combined with the fact that (s)he may never have set foot in that particular school or worked with that age student, the lack of lesson plans can be daunting.

Super Sub is a collection of activities which can be used with a variety of grade levels. Some of the ideas require little or no advance preparation, while others are best assembled and kept in a "ready bag" for the quick grab after that early-morning call from the school district. The first chapter outlines a number of games, which are good "ice breakers," especially if the classroom is self-contained and you find yourself working with the same students for the entire day. Likewise, if the sub assignment is for more than one day, you may wish to use a game during your first encounter with the students and proceed to more structured work on the second day.

Chapters two through four contain activities related to language arts, math, social studies, and science respectively. Most of these are easily implemented, requiring few materials and little preparation. Chapter five, "All About Them," provides a number of ways to involve the student on a personal level. The ideas in this chapter will give you insight into the lives and minds of the students. Preparing a sample based on yourself is a great way to encourage students to open up to you. Chapter six, "Picture Files," offers ways to use a preassembled collection of pictures, such as those clipped from magazines, newspapers, old calendars, greeting cards, etc.

Chapter seven, "Novel Ideas," and chapter eight, "Art," require forethought and some preparation. While "Novel Ideas" contains some suggestions for use with any story or book, the reproducible activities require the substitute to obtain copies of the stories and to read them in advance. ISBN numbers are given for ease in finding the pieces used. Most of these stories are quite short and so are easily used in a single class period. For the activities in chapter eight, it is sometimes necessary to gather materials in advance. It is also advisable to make the product once before attempting to have students create it, both to help you understand the process and to have a sample to show students.

Super Sub is designed to help make the job of substituting less stressful and easier to implement. Armed with activities such as these and a host of classroom management strategies (please see "Classroom Management: The Essence of Substitute Survival"), you should find yourself well prepared to tackle most any middle school classroom.

CLASSROOM MANAGEMENT:
The Essence of Substitute Survival

The substitute teacher is an odd idea indeed. In what other line of work is a person expected to be ready to address 20 or more children with whom they have no prior acquaintance, in a place they may never have been before, within an hour or two of notification? Not only does the job description include teaching (a number of grade levels and a variety of subjects), it also likely requires lunch, recess, or bus duty and mastery of the "lay of the land" in short order. How is one person to accomplish all this and actually provide a meaningful experience for the students to whom he or she has been assigned?

When teachers have been asked to define an effective substitute, responses often include the following: "someone who is confident," "someone with deep pockets," "someone who understands classroom logistics." The question that invariably follows from those who sub is "How can I learn to do/be all those things?"

Surviving, and even enjoying, the substitute experience is directly linked to the three areas alluded to by the teacher responses above: attitude, preparedness, and classroom management skills.

An effective substitute projects an attitude of confidence and capability. Students understand from the beginning that this teacher is the person in control and (s)he knows what (s)he is doing. To help formulate such an attitude, be as prepared as possible. Become familiar with the schools you have agreed to substitute for, visiting them in advance if possible. When you visit, meet the principal and note the essential features of the school, such as the location of the restrooms, lunchroom, computer room, gymnasium, library, xerox room, and office. Keep a "ready bag" of supplies and activities appropriate to the grade levels you teach. Read up on the ages with which you work, educating yourself about the typical social, emotional, and cognitive functioning of this age. If you have taken the time to organize yourself in this manner, you will feel much more relaxed and self-assured when you make your entrance into that great unknown.

Try to arrive at least 30 minutes early. This gives you an opportunity to survey the room, check out the lesson plans (or lack thereof), find the student roster, and organize your materials. If a seating chart has not been left by the teacher, note that this will be the first order of the day. Introduce yourself to a teacher in a nearby classroom, and ask if this person can be a guide should you need assistance during the day. Before students enter, write your name on the chalkboard and leave it there.

Once students arrive, introduce yourself. The next task is to take roll and/or make a seating chart. You may wish to enlist a student who is eager to be helpful to accomplish this. As you

take roll, walk around the room and establish eye contact with the students. Say, "Mike Smith" and when Mike says, "Here," find his eyes, smile, and reply, "Hello, Mike."
Once roll is taken, a good way to "break the ice" is to tell a story about yourself. Perhaps you have visited an interesting landmark or part of the country. Maybe you can relate an anecdote that students would enjoy. Or you might just tell students a little about your history and why you have landed in this part of the country or in this city.

As you proceed with the lessons of the day, keep in mind that students will constantly be testing you. Expect them to make comments or attempt ploys they would not contemplate with the regular teacher. Maintain a sense of humor. Rather than becoming flustered, angry, or dictatorial, reach for a way to smile at the impish behavior. If you catch an off-color joke or remark being whispered around, you might smile and say something like, "That's probably something you should tell your friend at recess" or "I didn't really hear you say that, did I?" The student response will most likely be "no," at which time you can reply, "Oh good, I thought not." Of course, everyone knows you heard it, but by treating it in this way, you have let them know that you know what's going on but that they aren't going to get much of a reaction out of you. What you are attempting to do is instill respect, but not fear, and promote an attitude of cooperation. If you can set this tone, managing the day will be much easier.

Having come to your position with confidence and organization, then, what else can you use to "stack the deck" in your favor? The following are some classroom management strategies which may assist you:

- Keep students actively involved in activities. The passive student will find a way to occupy him/herself, and it may not be a way you find desirable.
- To quiet students and reestablish control after recess, lunch, or an exciting activity, read a story, dim the lights, or pull the shades.
- Ask if the teacher has a signal for quiet. This may be flicking the lights, holding up a hand, ringing a bell, etc.
- Note potential problem students right away. Enlist their help, make them your allies and you will likely avoid greater difficulties.
- Move disruptive students if necessary. Placing them in the front of the room or near the teacher's desk may be helpful. Avoid threatening to send them to the office. You want to maintain control within the room as much as possible. The office should be a last resort.
- Go with the flow. If something isn't working, or students are unable to function productively in an activity, change it. Don't be afraid to use your own judgment about what a particular group can handle.

Maintaining a positive, upbeat attitude, arriving well prepared, and remaining flexible and animated are often the keys to substitute success. With experience, you will gather your own repertoire of activities and methods that work best for you, eventually becoming the *Super Sub* you were meant to be!

Games

Teacher-Directed Activities

Games provide an easy way to get students involved in a variety of activities. Through games, rapport between yourself and students is easily established. Students will also become actively engaged in learning, and classroom management issues are, therefore, often diminished. In this chapter you will find a number of games pertaining to different subjects and appropriate for several grades.

Fixes

This game is designed to give practice in identifying and using prefixes and suffixes. Prepare the cards necessary for the game in advance, or ask students to make them. Before beginning this game, lead a short discussion about what prefixes and suffixes are. Write examples of each on the board and leave them there during the game.

1. Using 3" x 5" cards, print different prefixes and suffixes on the front of the cards. On the back, print the word "prefix" or "suffix." Example:

UN	prefix
front of card	back of card

2. Divide the class into two teams. Then arrange nine desks in a tic-tac-toe formation.

3. Playing the game:
   Students stand in two lines on opposite sides of the desks. Hold up a card and show the front and the back of it to the first player on team one. He or she must supply a word that uses that prefix. If the response is correct, the player chooses one of the nine desks at which to sit. If the response is incorrect, the first player on the opposite team tries to supply a correct response. The game continues in this fashion until one of the teams scores a tic-tac-toe line. Keep score on the board for both teams. Play continues until a set point value or time limit is reached.

Singular, Plural, Possessive

Knowing when to use an apostrophe is always a difficult concept. This game offers students an interesting way to practice this skill. Prepare the dice necessary for this game in advance, or ask students to make them. Before beginning the game, lead a short discussion about using apostrophes. Write the following chart on the board and leave it there during the game. Ask students to give several other examples for the chart before you begin playing the game. Include some irregular plurals and possessives as well as regular ones.

Singular	Singular Possessive	Plural	Plural Possessive
cat	cat's	cats	cats'
person	person's	people	people's
wife	wife's	wives	wives'
box	box's	boxes	boxes'

The cube masters for this game are found on pages 9 and 10.

1. Divide students into two or three teams. Each team will make three picture cubes. Only one "possessive" cube is needed for the entire class.

2. Using the picture cube master on page 9, ask each group to draw pictures of things on each face of the cube. Students should also write the name of the noun on each face, checking the spelling of the words with you when necessary. Next, direct students to cut out the cubes and mount them on construction paper for backing. Then tape the ends together. It is a good idea to have several extra picture cube masters to allow for mistakes. Requirements for each cube are as follows:
   - One face must contain a picture of a word whose plural uses "es" (such as box)
   - One face must contain a picture of a word whose plural is a completely different word (such as person-people)
   - All pictures must be of nouns

3. While students do this, make the "possessive" cube found on page 10.

4. When the cubes are completed, collect them and ask students to move to desks so that their team members are sitting together.

5. Playing the game:
   Hand the first player on team one a picture cube and the "possessive" cube. He or she throws both cubes. The picture cube gives the word that must be used and the "possessive" cube gives the direction to be followed. For example, if the picture cube shows a "bus" and the possessive cube comes up "plural possessive," the student must go to the board and write the plural possessive of "bus" (buses'). If he or she does this correctly, the team scores one point. If the student can then use the plural possessive form of that word correctly in a sentence, the team receives an extra point. If the student

is unable to write the correct form of the word, play passes to the next team, who has the option of trying that word or throwing for a new word. As the game progresses, vary the picture cubes. Play continues until a set point value or time limit is reached.

Special Notes:
- You may wish to help with spelling or make correct spelling a rule of the game.
- When the word "FREE" shows up on the possessive cube, the student may choose one of the four options and receives the following points for a correct response: singular-1 point, plural-2 points, singular possessive-3 points, plural possessive-4 points. One extra point for using the word in a sentence is also given.

Nyms

Using homonyms, synonyms, and antonyms can be a great way to have fun with words and improve vocabulary. For this game, it is probably best to make cards in advance, but if you have enough time, it can be educational for students to create them instead. Twenty cards each of homonyms, synonyms, and antonyms are suggested. On the front of each card, write a word, and on the back of the card, write "homonym," "synonym," or "antonym."

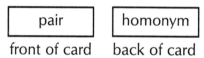

front of card   back of card

1. Once the cards are made, shuffle them so that the homonyms, synonyms, and antonyms are mixed together.

2. Divide students into two or three teams and ask them to move to desks so that their team members are sitting together.

3. Playing the game:
   The first player on team one draws a card. That player has ten seconds to respond with a correct answer. If a correct answer is given within the time allowed, the team scores one point. The student may then give a sentence using the word correctly. If the sentence is correct, the team scores another point. If a correct response is not given to the word card or time elapses, the word passes to the next team. If all teams miss the word, a new word is drawn as play passes back to the first team. Play continues until a set point value or time limit is reached.

Puzzlers

This game can be played using any subject area. You will need to bring about five pieces of large poster board with you for students to use in creating this game. Cut the poster boards into four pieces each. You will also need thick magic markers.

1. Students work in pairs. Each pair receives a piece of poster board.

2. Instruct students to draw a picture of something they are studying in _____ (choose a subject). Once the picture is drawn, ask them to write a question about it.

3. After the picture and question are finished, each pair needs to draw puzzle pieces onto their poster board. You may want to give a minimum and maximum number of pieces, such as not less than 10 or no more than 20. Students then need to cut out the puzzle pieces.

4. Playing the game:
   Once all the pieces are cut out, pairs exchange puzzles. At your signal, they begin to put the puzzles together. Students who complete the puzzle within one minute receive 50 points, two minutes 40 points, three minutes 30 points, four minutes 20 points, five minutes 10 points. When all the puzzles are assembled, each pair has a chance to answer the question. If they do so correctly, they receive 10 bonus points.

Function Machine

This game can be played with almost any grade level. It can be used to develop and reinforce mathematical thinking on many levels. Before beginning this game, draw a "function machine" on the board. Show how numbers enter (input), are processed, and exit (output). Keep this diagram on the board during the game. Ask students to give several function examples and input/output numbers before you begin playing the game.

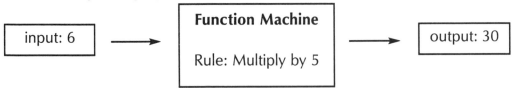

| input: 6 | → | **Function Machine**

Rule: Multiply by 5 | → | output: 30 |

1. Ask students to sit in a circle. Begin by being "IT" yourself. Think of a math function, such as "add 10." (It is a good idea to use an easy example at first.) When you have a rule in mind, say, "I'm thinking of a math function."

2. Playing the game:
   Choose someone to begin by giving you a number. (You may want to limit the span of the numbers used, such as numbers under 100.) Mentally, perform the function and give the output number. For example, if your rule was "add 10" and the student said "54,"

you would reply "64." The next student in the circle now gives you a new number and you give the output. When students think they know the function rule, they must raise their hands and wait to be called on. If they are correct, they become "IT" and must think of a new function rule. If they are incorrect, continue accepting input numbers and giving output numbers until someone guesses the function correctly.

Special Notes
- In order to give slower students a better chance, it is a good idea to establish a minimum number of input-output numbers that must be given before guesses are taken. You may wish to require at least three to five before you allow guesses.
- For more advanced students, more complicated functions may be used, such as $3x + 5$.
- Depending on the level of students or the complexity of the functions, you may wish to allow students to use scratch paper during the game.

Guide to Reproducibles

Treasure Hunt for Comparisons

This game asks students to find examples of similes and metaphors in literature. Before starting to play, explain similes and metaphors. Stress that both of these language tools are ways of comparing unlike ideas in order to make a point. Use the student handout on page 11 to help make these terms more clear. After students complete the handout, discuss their answers and be certain that they have understood what things are being compared in each sentence.

1. Divide the class into two teams. Within the teams, students will work in pairs.

2. Pass out books or ask students to choose a novel. Each pair can work with a different book or story.

3. Each pair will also need a paper and pencil.

4. Ask students to divide their paper into two columns and to label one "Similes" and the other "Metaphors."

5. Playing the game:
Explain to students that when you give the signal, they will begin to search their books for phrases that contain similes and metaphors. One person can hunt while the other records. Tell them they do not need to write the entire sentence, only the phrase that contains the simile or metaphor. Set a time limit, perhaps five minutes, and let students begin. Once time is called, ask each pair to read their list of similes and metaphors aloud. You are the judge who will determine whether a phrase is categorized properly. Each pair receives one point for each properly identified phrase. The team with the most points is the winner.

Tips, Please

This game can be used to provide practice with decimals and percents. Using a black magic marker, write 10%, 15%, and 20% on three pieces of paper large enough so that the numbers can be seen by everyone. Place these face down on your desk. Also prepare 20 price cards which have dollar amounts written on them in black marker. Use only even dollar amounts (no cents).

1. Use the student worksheet on page 12 to help students understand how to find 10%, 15%, and 20% of a number. Once they understand the concept, divide them into three teams. Each team needs scrap paper, clean paper to record answers on, and a black or dark-colored marker. Within each team, students should pair up. Make one group of three if there is an odd number of students on a team.

2. Playing the game:
   The first two students in each team step to the front of their line with paper and marker. The teacher then turns over one percent card and one price card. All three pairs work to find the answer. When they think they have the answer, they write it on a piece of paper and hold it up for the teacher to see. The first pair to determine the correct amount receives 1 point. Play can continue for a specified amount of time or until one team receives a predetermined number of points. Percent and price cards can be shuffled and reused as the game goes on.

   Note: To make computing answers easy for yourself, keep a calculator on the desk to have the correct answer ready for each problem.

"Check" It Out

This game offers practices with a variety of math skills in real-life applications. It can be played individually or in pairs. Before passing out the student handout on page 13, discuss the use of checks with students. Ask them to name some things for which their parents write checks.

1. Pass out the handout and ask someone to read the first paragraph.

2. Copy the first entry from the sample check register onto the board. Go through the purchases for which check numbers 100-102 were used and show students how to subtract the check amount to get the running balance.

3. Next, ask someone to read the second paragraph on the handout, which explains the game. Ask students if they understand how to play or have any questions.

4. Pass out six checks and a check register form to each student (or pair). These masters are found on pages 14 and 15. Draw a large sample of a check on the board. If possible, use one color of chalk to draw the check and another color to fill it in. Show students how to fill in the check.

5. Playing the game:
   When you give the signal to begin, students will choose purchases from the list of "possible purchases" on their handout and write checks for these. They should keep a record of these purchases in the check register and compute the running balance each time they purchase something. The person (or pair) to spend as much money as possible without going over the $200.00 is the winner.

   When time is called, or everyone has finished, ask for final balances from students. You will need to check the potential winners' subtraction for accuracy.

   Note: You may wish to set a time limit, and this will vary according to the age of the students. You may also wish to allow the use of calculators, but all students should have access to them if they are used.

Vocabulary Bingo

This game can be played using any subject area and is useful for reinforcing vocabulary. You will need to bring one package of large index cards (4" x 6") and two packages of small index cards for students to use in creating this game. You will also need something to use as counters. These are easily made by cutting construction paper into small squares.

1. To create the game pieces, students will work in pairs. Distribute small index cards to each pair. Direct students to look through the current chapter of a certain text and write down 10-20 vocabulary words and their definitions, placing one word on the front of each small index card and its definition on the back of that index card. Social studies and science texts or vocabulary words from an English lesson or a novel under study work well.

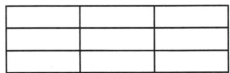

2. Next, give each student one large index card. Have him or her divide the card into nine equal sections (three across and three down). Following this, each student chooses nine vocabulary words and writes one word in each square of the index card. Although some words may be the same on different cards, no two cards should be exactly alike, nor contain exactly the same words. These are the bingo cards.

3. Place students in groups of five or six. One student will be the caller. He or she collects a complete set of vocabulary cards, making certain that there is a vocabulary card for every word on the bingo cards. Students exchange bingo cards in the group so that they do not have the card they made as a playing card.

4. Playing the game:
   Just as in regular bingo, the caller calls out the vocabulary word. The caller chooses one person who has the word on his/her card to define the word. If the chosen person defines it correctly, he/she gets to cover it and no one else gets to cover it. If the player does not define it correctly, all students who have the word on their cards get to cover it. If no one has the word on his/her card, a student may ask to define it. (If several students volunteer, the caller chooses one.) If the player is correct, he/she may cover any word on his/her card. Play continues until someone has a completely covered card. The "winner" then becomes the caller for the next game.

Picture Cube

Possessive Cube

	Plural	
Singular	**Free**	**Singular Possessive**
	Plural Possessive	
	Free	

Similes and Metaphors

For use with "Treasure Hunt for Comparisons"

Similes and metaphors show similarities between two things or ideas that are not really very much alike. They do this in different ways.

A simile compares things through the use of *like* or *as*. For example:

> Her mother was **as lovely as** a rose.
> Her mother was **like** a rose, beautiful and elegant.

A metaphor compares things **directly**, often using a state of being verb, such as *is, are, was,* or *were*. For example:

> Her mother **was** a rose.

In the examples above, the two things that are being compared are the mother and the rose. With the use of either the simile or the metaphor, the reader understands that the mother is similar to a rose—that she is pretty and stylish. That is the purpose of this type of figurative language: to give the reader an image that helps in making the picture more clear. Similes can be made into metaphors and metaphors can be made into similes.

Decide whether the sentences below use similes or metaphors. Write "S" or M" on the line to the left of each one. Then write what the simile or metaphor is comparing on the blanks below each sentence.

_____ 1. The wind brushed against his face gently like the breath of a small child.
_____ is being compared to _____

_____ 2. She was a devil.
_____ is being compared to _____

_____ 3. As slowly as a turtle, the boy walked up to the chalkboard.
_____ is being compared to _____

_____ 4. Suddenly, the children were birds, flying free within the fantasy of their minds.
_____ are being compared to _____

_____ 5. Like a bird, the young girl's spirit soared.
_____ is being compared to _____

Tips, Please

You may be aware that your parents leave a tip for waiters and waitresses in restaurants. The amount of a tip is supposed to reflect the quality of the service you received from the waiter or waitress. If service is adequate, the standard tip amount is 15% of the final bill. If you are not happy with the service, however, you may choose to leave only 10% (or less). On the other hand, if you feel that the service was superior, you might leave 20% (or more).

Here is an easy way to figure out the tip amount you wish to leave by using mental math. Start with 10%. This is easy because **taking 10% of a dollar amount just means moving the decimal point to the left one space.** For example:

    1. 10% Of $10.00 = $1.00   2. 10% of $25.00 = $2.50

If you wish to leave 15%, figure out what 10% would be, take half of that amount, and add the two together. In the examples above, 15% would be:

    1. 10% Of $10.00 = $1.00   Half of $1.00 = .50 $1.00 + .50 = $1.50
        Answer: 15% of $10.00 = $1.50

    2. 10% of $25.00 = $2.50   Half of $2.50 = $1.25 $2.50 + $1.25 = $3.75
   Answer: 15% of $25.00 = $3.75

If you wish to leave 20%, figure out what 10% would be and double it. In the examples above, 20% would be:

    1. 10% of $10.00 = $1.00   2 x $1.00 = $2.00
        Answer: 20% of $10.00 = $2.00

    2. 10% of $25.00 = $2.50   2 x $2.50 = $5.00
        Answer: 20% of $25.00 = $5.00

Fill in the chart below. Use mental math to figure each percent.

Dollar Amount	10%	15%	20%
$23.00			
$65.00			
$48.00			

"Check" It Out

Many people have a checking account into which they deposit money. Often, when they make purchases, they write checks for them instead of using cash. They keep track of the balance in their checking account by keeping a check register like the one on this page.

Your teacher will give you six checks with which to purchase some items of your choice. You may purchase each item only once. You will begin with a balance of $200.00 in your checking account. Each time you write a check, you will need to subtract the check amount from your balance and enter a new balance. Make certain that you do not spend more money than you have, or the bank will bounce your check (send it back to you) AND charge you a $25.00 returned-check fee!

The person who spends as much money as possible without going over the $200.00 is the winner.

Sample Check Register:

Check Number	Date	Description (written to)	Amount of check	Amount of deposit	Balance $200.00
100	2/9/01	Mike's Grocery	$45.67		154.33
101	2/11/01	Town Cleaners	13.35		140.98
102	2/11/01	Sportsmania	78.23		62.75

Possible Purchases:

Jeans $36.11	Tickets to Disneyland $72.50
Groceries $51.29	Tennis Racket $82.36
Video Game Rental $10.15	Sweatshirt $25.91
Pizza $12.37	Ice Cream $5.46 Skateboard $38.03
Movie Passes $15.00	Hamburgers-to-Go Lunch $7.62

Check No. _____   Date _____

Pay to the
Order of _____ $ [   ]

_____ Dollars

Education Bank

For _____   _____

:842165 : 0602   312968

Check No. _____   Date _____

Pay to the
Order of _____ $ [   ]

_____ Dollars

Education Bank

For _____   _____

:842165 : 0602   312968

Check No. _____   Date _____

Pay to the
Order of _____ $ [   ]

_____ Dollars

Education Bank

For _____   _____

:842165 : 0602   312968

Check Register Form

Check Number	Date	Description (written to)	Amount of check	Amount of deposit	Balance $200.00
100					
101					
102					
103					
104					
105					
106					
107					
108					
109					

Check Register Form

Check Number	Date	Description (written to)	Amount of check	Amount of deposit	Balance $200.00
100					
101					
102					
103					
104					
105					
106					
107					
108					
109					

The activities in this chapter require the student to listen, write, read, research, act, and create. Many of these ideas begin with observable and experiential activities to provide students with concrete situations upon which they can expand.

Bag of Tricks

For this activity, you may want to assemble some items in advance, or you can choose some from the classroom. Place five to ten items in a bag. Put these phrases on the board: A) a murder case, B) a movie, C) an accident. Blindfold each student and instruct them to draw something out of the bag. It does not matter if some students draw out the same items. Once everyone has drawn an item, tell them that the object they drew is a key element in a story about one of the three phrases on the board. They are to choose one of these ideas and write a story which involves the object they drew from the bag.

The Sub in Grade X

Ask students to place themselves into the role of news reporter for the city newspaper. The assignment is to get the "inside scoop" on the substitute in grade _____. They need to write ten questions they would like to ask you, leaving room for answers under each question. As you answer, they should record your responses. They may also jot down notes from other students' questions. When the "interview" has been completed, each student can write a news article on "The Sub in Grade _____." When students have completed their articles, ask for volunteers to share their writing with the class.

Will the Real Substitute Stand Up?

Bring in ten photos of different people, one of which is a picture of you at a young age. Mount the pictures on a poster board with a number under each photo. Let students view the photos for a few minutes and then ask them to write the number of the photo they think is you. They must also write the reasons for their choice. Next, write the numbers of the photos on the board and ask students which picture they chose by asking for a show of hands. Ask some of the students to share the reasons for their choices. Once all the guesses have been recorded, tell them which picture is actually of you. Then ask them to write a paragraph about how you have changed since the photo was taken.

Songs

Bring the lyrics of a favorite song to class with you to copy for students. Before beginning to discuss your song, ask students to name some of their favorite songs. Ask why these are their favorites. Explain that one of the reasons songs are enjoyed by so many people is that their words (called *lyrics*) speak to the listener. Continue to explain that songs are really poetry put to music. Because they are poetry, they often contain many poetic tools. Then pass out the lyrics of the song you brought with you. Enlist students' help in analyzing the song for rhyme scheme, the use of a refrain or chorus, imagery, and themes. You will find a short definition of each of these terms in the answer key of this book. Following this, ask students to work in pairs to write the lyrics to a song of their own. Rap music lends itself well to this activity and is something with which many students are familiar.

Comic Mad Libs

Divide students into groups of six. Ask each group to choose a scribe, or appoint one. Go around to each group and point to each student in succession asking "who" to the first one, "what" to the second one, "when" to the third one, "where" to the fourth one, "why" to the fifth one, and "how" to the sixth one. The result will be a humorous "mad lib" sentence. Once each group has its sentence, ask students to create a six-block comic strip which illustrates the 5 "W's" and "H" which they supplied. Comic strips can be drawn and illustrated on construction paper. They do not need to contain words. Ask students to share their work with the class when they are finished.

Describe and Draw

Ask students to create a monster by generating a list of characteristics (such as four triangle heads, ten lollipop feet, a square body, etc.). On another sheet of paper, ask them to draw their monster. The name of the monster should appear at the top of both the description and the drawing. Next, ask students to turn over their drawing and exchange their descriptions with a classmate. The classmate will then draw the monster based on the description given to him/her. Once completed, compare the similarities and differences in the two drawings and discuss why the monsters are not exactly alike.

Movie Set

Before distributing the student sheet for this exercise, discuss the climax of a story, book, or movie. Explain to students that the climax is the most exciting part of the story, often called the *turning point* of the story. In a movie, the climax is almost always signaled by music. Ask students to identify the climax of a few of their favorite films and to explain how they knew that scene was the climax. Then pass out the activity sheet on page 20. Students may work in pairs or alone to complete this activity.

Dictionary Delirium

Look through a dictionary and assign to each student a word that is likely to be unknown by that person. Using the student handout on page 21, discuss the sample entry at the top of the page and make certain that students understand all the different parts and symbols involved in the entry. Students then write a dictionary entry according to what they think the word assigned to them means. Stress that they are to write a *dictionary entry*, like the sample at the top of the student page, not just meanings for the word. They will also draw a picture of the word. Following this, students can look up the actual dictionary entry and copy it onto the page. Ask students to share their work when finished. The pages can be collected to be made into a book at the end of the activity.

Cryptic Codes

Using the student handout on page 22, explain to students the process of making a cryptic code. Allow time for students to decode the example, assisting those who may be having trouble. Then choose a subject, such as science, social studies, or math, and ask students to write a sentence about what they have been studying in that subject. Students then need to create a cryptic code of their own and write the sentence in code. Once they are finished, they can exchange papers with a classmate and decode the message.

Imagine

The activity on page 23 will help students to think creatively about achieving a goal and to explain the process with definite reasons. Once students have finished their short essays, ask some of them to share their writing with the class. You may also ask them to draw a picture to accompany their work.

That's Just Nonsense!

Before using the student page, write the basic parts of speech and an example of each on the board (noun—*Bill*, verb—*yelled*, adjective—*tall*, adverb—*loudly*, preposition—*around*, conjunction—*and*). Discuss them briefly. Ask students to give other examples of each type. Then hand out the activity on page 24. When students finish, ask them to share some of their words and sentences with the class.

Movie Set

Below are the plots for several movies. Work with a partner to write a scene which might show the climax of the film. When you are finished writing, act out your scene for the rest of the class.

an F.B.I. agent must prevent a dangerous weapon from entering the United States

an injured wild animal is rescued by a child

a surprise avalanche traps two friends under the snow

a young wizard must save his land from evil

a child who is in an accident must learn to cope with a permanent disability

in a future time, children are raised by computers

Name _____

 # Dictionary Delirium

Below is a dictionary entry. Notice that it tells you how to say the word **(kur'ənt)**, what part of speech the word is *(adj.)* and *(n.)* , what language the word came from [< L. *currere,* to run], and several meanings of the words (1-3 as **adj.** and 1-3 as **n.**) At the very end of the entry, other forms of the word are given **(curr'rent•ly adv.)**

current (kur'ənt) adj. [< L. *currere,* to run] **1.** now going on; of the present time **2.** circulating **3.** commonly accepted; prevalent --**n. 1.** a flow of water or air in a definite direction **2.** a general tendency **3.** the flow or rate of flow of electricity in a conductor —**curr'rent•ly adv.**

_____
Your Word

Your Dictionary Entry:

_____
_____
_____
_____
_____
_____
_____

Picture

Actual Dictionary Entry:

_____
_____
_____
_____
_____

Cryptic Codes

Cryptic codes can be made by changing the letters of the alphabet so that they stand for other letters. Here is an example:

A = B	F = G	K = L	P = Q	U = V	Z = A
B = C	G = H	L = M	Q = R	V = W	
C = D	H = I	M = N	R = S	W = X	
D = E	I = J	N = O	S = T	X = Y	
E = F	J = K	O = P	T = U	Y = Z	

Using the above code, the following message can be written:

DSZQUJD   DPEFT   BSF   GVO!

Can you decode it? Write the letter that each coded letter stands for above the code. Look in the column on the right for the coded letter and write the letter on the left to decode it.

C R
D S Z Q U J D   D P E F T   B S F G V O!

After you decode the sample, make up your own cryptic code and write a sentence about something you have been studying. Then see if a classmate can decode your message.

A =	F =	K =	P =	U =	Z =
B =	G =	L =	Q =	V =	
C =	H =	M =	R =	W =	
D =	I =	N =	S =	X =	
E =	J =	O =	T =	Y =	

Your coded message: _____

_____

_____

_____

_____

_____

_____

Imagine

What would you like to

DISCOVER

INVENT

ELIMINATE

SUPPORT

CREATE

Choose one of the above and list on the lines below at least three ways you might accomplish your goal. An example of a topic: I would like to eliminate hunger for children in America. Then write a short essay about your topic which includes why you have chosen this goal and the steps you think you could take to make it happen.

_____

_____

_____

_____

_____

_____

That's Just Nonsense!

Look at the nonsense words below. Write a sentence for each word and then decide what part of speech you think the word would be if it were a real word. Parts of speech include noun, verb, adjective, adverb, preposition, and conjunction.

1. **snorber** _____
    Part of speech _____

2. **bruzzed** _____
    Part of speech _____

3. **dafolly** _____
    Part of speech _____

4. **hiderlada** _____
    Part of speech _____

5. **af** _____
    Part of speech _____

Now create five of your own nonsense words. Exchange papers with a classmate and ask him or her to write the sentences and tell what part of speech the word might be.

1. _____ _____
    Part of speech _____

2. _____ _____
    Part of speech _____

3. _____ _____
    Part of speech _____

4. _____ _____
    Part of speech _____

5. _____ _____
    Part of speech _____

Math Activities

Teacher-Directed Activities

There are many enjoyable ways to use math. In this chapter you will find a variety of math activities on a number of different concepts and levels. Use your own imagination to tailor them to your needs.

Math Facts Cards

Instead of using flash cards to reinforce math facts, bring an ordinary deck or two of playing cards with you to class. Depending on the level of the students, you can use these cards to add, subtract, or multiply (they will not work for division). Simply turn any two cards face up and ask a student to perform the desired operation with those two numbers. Make certain that the student reads the math sentence aloud. For example, if the two cards are 2 and 8 and the operation is subtract, the student needs to say, "8 minus 2 equals 6." If the student gets the correct answer, he or she may keep the cards. If not, either you keep them or return them to the bottom of the pile. A time limit of about five seconds to answer is suggested. Rename the face cards as you like, perhaps making jacks equal to 10, queens equal to 11, and kings equal to 12, or 10, 20, and 30 respectively. Jokers may be kept in as wild cards, with the student choosing the number to use.

Toothpick Towers

A favorite activity for almost any middle school student involves the challenge of creating the sturdiest toothpick structure. For this activity, you will need lots of toothpicks and either glue or sticky tack. (Sticky tack is less messy and easier to use.) Place students in pairs or groups of three with a pile of toothpicks and glue/sticky tack. Challenge them to see which group can make the sturdiest structure. Make certain that they understand what *sturdy* means before they start. Structures made from triangles will be the sturdiest and, hopefully, some groups will discover this on their own.

Two, Four, Six, Eight, What Can You Do with This License Plate?

Take students to the school parking lot or to an area where they can see car license plates. Ask them to copy down ten license plate numbers. Return to the room and write the following questions on the board:

1. What is the sum of the digits on each of your license plates? (If there are any letters, ignore them in the first four questions.)
2. What is the product of the digits on each of your license plates?
3. What is the result if you subtract the numbers on your license plates in order?
4. What is the result if you divide the numbers on your license plates in order?
5. Suppose that each number and/or letter on each license plate is part of a secret code. What message does each license plate carry?

Note: Depending on the level of the students, you may wish to provide calculators. You also may wish to make a chart (using the headings below) on which students can record their answers.

License Plate Number	Sum of Digits	Product of Digits	Subtraction of Digits	Division of Digits

Guide to Reproducibles

On Sale Today

This activity is useful for explaining the relationship of fractions, decimals, and percents. It provides practice in converting numbers from one of these forms to another. Given the scope of most curricula, it is probably more appropriate for grade six and above. To extend the activity, place prices and sale discounts around the room on various objects. Students may work in pairs to complete the worksheet on page 30. The use of calculators is highly recommended.

Don't Forget The Tax

To provide more realism for this activity, you may wish to bring along ten items tagged with the prices and tax rates listed in the chart on the student handout found on page 31. By working through the handout, students will be guided step-by-step in computing sales tax. Students may work in pairs to complete the activity sheet. Calculators are an option.

Survey, Graph, Report

For this activity, divide students into groups of about four students. Ask each group to write two questions to ask the class. These questions should begin with "How many students . . . " Examples might be "have pets" or "have been to Disney World." Choose ten of these questions to write on the board for the final survey. Next, ask students to answer the questions by a show of hands and record the number who answer affirmatively next to each question. Then pass out the student handout on page 32 to each student. Help students make a bar graph for the first two answers and then ask them to finish the rest of the graph. When everyone is finished, recreate the graph on the board. Following this, place the chart below on the board and ask students to copy it on a clean sheet of paper:

Question Number	No. of Students Answering "Yes"	Total in Class	Results as Fractions	Results as Percents
1	12	33	$\frac{12}{33}$	37%

Assist students in filling out their charts as in the sample shown here, and in making statements using the data. For example, "$\frac{12}{33}$, or 37%, of the class have pets." If you wish, students may work in pairs to complete this part of the activity. The use of calculators is highly recommended.

Pizza Party

This math activity reinforces fraction concepts. It is probably best played by students who have some knowledge of fractions, though they need not be able to perform operations with fractions. Distribute the student handouts on pages 33 and 34. Begin by going through the first problem with the class. Draw the pizza circle on the board. Ask a student to solve the problem by coming to the board to do the problem. Here is how the pizza should look:

1. Hungry Horsefly ordered ⅜ of a pizza. He wants one piece with pepperoni and cheese and two pieces with black olives and cheese.

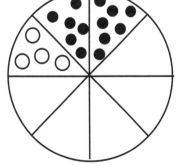

Once the problem has been solved and the pizza drawn correctly, go over the process with students as follows:

Step 1: The number of pieces you need to divide the pizza into is show by the bottom number, or denominator, of the fraction. Begin by cutting the pizza into this number of pieces.

Step 2: The number of pieces ordered is shown by the top number, or numerator, of the fraction.

Step 3: Decorate the number of pieces ordered with the items that were requested.

Following this explanation, students can complete the worksheets. Encourage them to use markers or crayons to color the pizzas.

Palindromic Fun

Palindromes are numbers, words, or phrases that say the same thing forward as they do backward. Examples include "131," "Dad," and the sentence "Madam, I'm Adam." Palindromes are interesting to explore, both in language and in math. The activity sheet on page 35 gives examples of palindromes and shows how to turn any number into a palindromic number. Students usually enjoy the challenge of discovering how many steps it takes before a number becomes a palindrome.

Inches, Feet, or Yards?

This activity is useful for practice in estimating and calculating actual measurement. It also allows students to move around the room, which provides a good break from seatwork. Using the student handout on page 36, help students to begin. You will want to have rulers and yardsticks (if possible) on hand. When they are finished with the activity, students can use dictionaries, encyclopedias, or computers to look up the lengths or heights of the items at the bottom of the page.

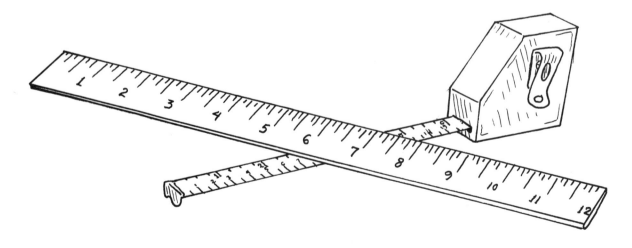

Lucky Dice

For this experiment, you will need 10-15 dice. If these are not available, use the "picture cube" master on page 9 of this book and direct students to write the numbers 1-6 on the cube, one number to a face. Then they can cut it out, tape it together, and use it as a die. The student handouts on pages 37 and 38 explain basic probability. Help students to perform a simple probability experiment with the die. Before dividing students into pairs for the experiment, read the first paragraph to the class. Ask them to give other examples of probability to see if they understand the concept. You might ask for the probability of getting a queen (any queen) in a deck of cards (4 out of 52, or 1 out of 13) versus the probability of getting a queen of clubs (1 out of 52). Once students have completed the experiment, compare each pair's results with what probability would predict should happen. (Each number would come up roughly the same number of times, about 16 or 17.) List each pair's results on the board and decide as a class whether, in general (on the average), probability theory holds true. If it does not, ask students to hypothesize what factors could have affected the outcome of the throws. Some factors would include the construction of the die (possible weighting), the way it was thrown, and the surface it landed on.

Imaginary Measurements

This creative math activity asks students to consider the idea of measurement and to understand calibration (though this term is not introduced). After students complete the handout on page 39, ask them to share some of their responses with the class and discuss whether their guesses seem reasonable. For example, if someone said that a goldfish would use a fin as a unit of measure and then said the creature's length was 2000 fins long, this would not be a reasonable estimate.

On Sale Today

Stores often advertise their products for sale by using fractions or percents. Many times you will see signs that say "⅓ Off" or "50% Sale." Figuring out what such discounts mean can be challenging. It's important to know that fractions, decimals, and percents are all ways of saying the same thing. Here is how they can be converted:

1. To change a **fraction into a decimal,** divide the numerator by the denominator.
   Example: ⁵⁄₁₀ = 5 ÷ 10 = .50
2. To change a **decimal into a percent,** multiply it by 100.
   Example: .50 x 100 = 50%
3. To change a **decimal back into a fraction,** write it as the numerator and use the last place value of the decimal as the denominator.
   Example: .3 = ³⁄₁₀   .45 = ⁴⁵⁄₁₀₀   .356 = ³⁵⁶⁄₁₀₀₀
4. To change a **percent back into a decimal,** divide it by 100.
   Example: 50 ÷ 100 = .50

Use a calculator to fill in the chart below. The first one has been done for you.

Fraction	(Num + Den) =	Decimal	Dec x 100 =	Percent
½	1 ÷ 2 =	.50	.50 x 100 =	50%
		.25		
¾				
				35%
		.70		

You can use the above relationships to find the amount of discount and the sale price of items that are on sale. To do this, follow the steps below. The first one has been done for you.

1. Convert the discount into a decimal (25 ÷ 100 = .25).
2. Multiply the original price by the discount ($35.00 x .25).
3. Subtract the amount of the discount from the original price to find the sale price ($35.00 - $8.25 = $26.75).

Item	Discount	Original Price	Amt. of Discount	Sale Price
Jeans	25% off	$35.00	$8.75	$26.25
T-Shirt	⅓ off	$22.00		
Tennis Shoes	50% off	$75.00		
CD Player	¼ off	$150.00		
Skateboard	33% off	$85.00		

Don't Forget the Tax

Most of the time when you buy things, the total amount is different from the price marked on the item. This is because of the sales tax. Sales tax is an amount of money that is added to the cost of the item because the store must give some of the money it makes to the government. Taxes are used by our government to help pay for public projects such as parks and highways and for public employees.

Computing the amount of tax is easy if you understand the relationship of percents and decimals. They are just two ways of saying the same thing. Taxes are usually reported as a percent. To find the amount of the tax, follow the steps shown in the example below:

Tax rate: 4%   Item cost: $25.15

1. Change the percent back into a decimal by dividing it by 100.
   4 ÷ 100 = .04

2. Multiply the item cost by the decimal to find the amount of the tax.
   $25.15 x .04 = $1.01

3. Add the amount of the tax to the cost of the item to find the total price.
   $25.15 + $1.01 = $26.16

Use a calculator to fill in the chart below. The first one has been done for you.

Original Price	Tax Rate	Decimal (Tax Rate ÷ 100)	Amount of Tax (Item Cost x Dec.)	Total Price (Orig. Price + Tax)
$35.99	5%	5 ÷ 100 = .05	35.99 x .05 = 1.80	35.99 + 1.80 = $37.79
$103.68	10%			
$5.52	4%			
$243.25	7%			
$26.75	8%			
$98.31	15%			
$12.44	6%			
$7.37	12%			
$525.26	6%			

Survey, Graph, Report

After your class survey has been recorded on the board by the teacher, use the information to record the results on the bar graph below.

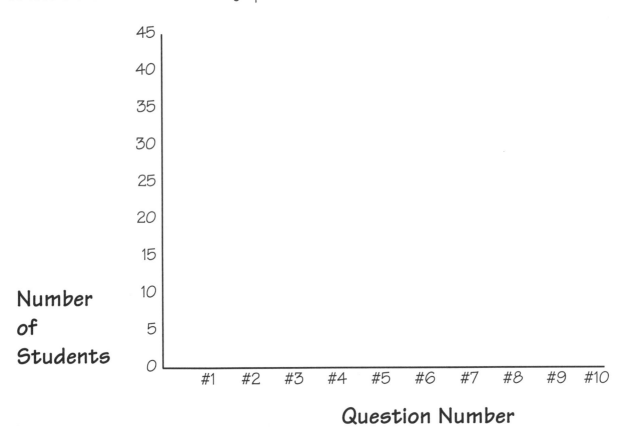

Now that you have reported these results in a graph, report them in two other ways, using fractions and percents. Use a separate piece of paper to make these lists.

To report the results as fractions, make the question into a statement. Then use the number of students who said "yes" as the numerator and the total number of students in the class as the denominator. For example, if the question was, "How many students have pets?" and the answer was "15 out of 32 students," the fraction would be $^{15}/_{32}$. The statement would be "$^{15}/_{32}$ of the class have pets."

To change the fraction into a percent, divide the numerator by the denominator and multiply that answer by 100. In the example above, $15 \div 32 = .47 \times 100 = 47\%$. The statement using the percent would be "47% of the students have pets."

Pizza Party

Pizzazz Pizza has to deliver pizza to the insects of the world. Because they are so small, however, the insects order fractions of pizzas, instead of whole ones. Cut each pizza into the correct number of pieces for each order. Then create the type of pizza ordered on the number of pieces that should be delivered to each insect.

1. Hungry Horsefly ordered ⅜ of a pizza. He wants 1 piece with pepperoni and cheese and 2 pieces with black olives and cheese.

2. Greedy Grasshopper wants ⅚ of a pizza. He ordered 3 pieces with onions and green pepper and the rest with pepperoni and black olives.

3. The Famished Fireflies are having a picnic. They ordered 2 and ⁵⁄₁₂ pizzas. They asked for all the pizzas to be divided into twelfths. On half of the first pizza, they would like pepperoni only. On the other half, they asked for just cheese. The second pizza was to be ⅓ black olives, ⅓ green pepper and onions, and ⅓ mushrooms. The rest should be topped with everything.

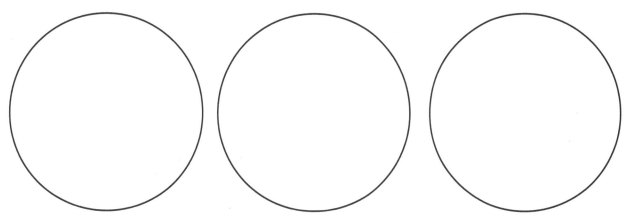

4. Munchy Mosquito has ordered ⁷⁄₁₆ of a pizza. He would like 3 pieces with pineapple and ham and the rest with pepperoni.

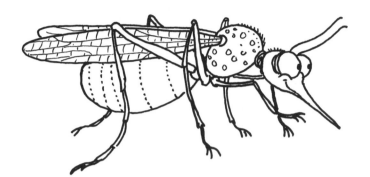 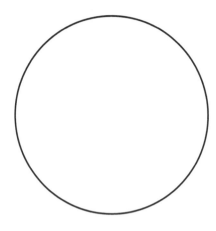

Now write two of your own Pizzazz Pizza orders for insects. Exchange them with a classmate and try to fill each other's orders correctly. Draw your own circles for each pizza and divide each one into the number of pieces required. Then draw the items ordered on each piece.

Order #1

Order #2

Palindromic Fun

Look at the numbers, words, and phrases below.

| 131 | Dad | 2002 | Mom | 10901 |

Madam, I'm Adam!

How are all of these things alike? _____

_____

Did you discover that they are the same forward as they are backward? Words, phrases, and numbers that have this special quality are called *palindromes*. The interesting thing about numbers is that any number can be made into a palindrome. Follow these steps to see how this is done.

1. Choose any number.
2. Add the number and the reverse of its digits together.
3. Continue step 2 until the number becomes a palindrome.

Examples:
```
  24              59
+ 42             +95
  66  1-step     154
      palindrome +451
                 605
                +506
                1111  3-step palindrome
```

See how many steps it takes to make these numbers into palindromes. Then try some of your own.

64   1234

    122   409

        3267   78

Inches, Feet, or Yards?

Choose the unit of measure you think would be **most appropriate** to measure the items below. Then make a guess about its **length (or height).** Finally, measure the item and record its true length/height.

Item	Unit of Measure (Guess)	Length (Guess)	Unit of Measure Used	Length (Actual)
your thumb				
desktop				
chalkboard				
pencil				
board eraser				
book				
height of wall				
door				
your height				
paper clip				

After your work with measuring above, what kind of guesses would you make for the following:

> length of a blue whale
> height of the Empire State Building
> height of a giraffe
> length of: an earthworm,
>   a peanut,
>   a football
>   a pick-up truck

Choose one of the above and check its actual length or height by using a dictionary, encyclopedia, or computer.

Lucky Dice

This experiment is about probability. Probability tells you how likely something is to occur. Imagine that you have one blue, one red, and one yellow Lifesaver in your hand. You ask your friend to close his/her eyes and choose one. In this case, the probability of your friend choosing any of the colors is 1 out of 3. This is because there are 3 lifesavers in total and 1 of each color. With a normal die (one that is not weighted or somehow deformed), the probability of throwing any number is 1 out of 6. This is because there are 6 possibilities on the die, and you can get only 1 of them on any throw.

You and your partner will perform this experiment to find out if your die is a "normal" die or if it is one that is more likely to come up with a certain number. Throw the die 50 times and have your partner record the number that comes up each time. Then have your partner throw the die 50 times while you record the number that comes up each time. Be certain to shake the die in your hand before each throw. On a separate sheet of paper, make a recording chart like the abbreviated example shown below. Place an "X" under the number that is thrown each time. When you are finished, put the totals for each number at the bottom of each column. The totals should add up to 100.

Probability theory would predict that each number would be thrown equally. This means that you should throw each number between 16 and 17 times out of 100 throws.

Number Showing on Die

Throw Number	1	2	3	4	5	6		
1		X						
2				X				
3						X		
•								
•								
•								
100			X					
Totals	8	12	25	18	30	7	=	100

Once you have these totals, you can draw some conclusions about this die. The probabilities of throwing a certain number for the die in the example above would be as follows:

P(1) = 8 out of 100   P(2) = 12 out of 100   P(3) = 25 out of 100
P(4) = 18 out of 100   P(5) = 30 out of 100   P(6) = 7 out of 100

Conclusions: You can see quickly that if you were using this die to play a game, you would be most likely to throw a 5 or 3, and more likely to throw a 4 or 2 than a 6 or 1.

Record the information you discovered about your die and answer the questions below.

P(1) = _____ out of 100   P(2) = _____ out of 100   P(3) = _____ out of 100
P(4) = _____ out of 100   P(5) = _____ out of 100   P(6) = _____ out of 100

What conclusions can you make about your die from the data you gathered?

_____

_____

_____

If you were playing a game with this die, would you have a fair chance or not? Explain your answer.

_____

_____

_____

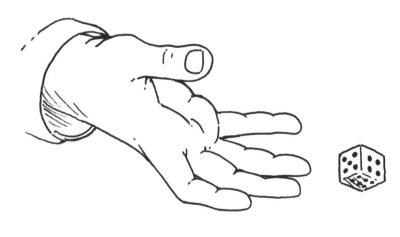

Name _____

 # Imaginary Measurements

Our units of measure are arbitrary. This means that someone made them up and people agreed to use the same units. In fact, measurement is not the same around the world, or the same for everything. The United States commonly uses inches, feet, yards, gallons, quarts, and pints, while most of the rest of the world uses the metric system.

The point is that anything can be used to measure things. Look at the chart below and decide what your "yardstick" would be if you were the type of being listed. Then fill in the rest of the chart according to your imaginary yardstick.

Being	Unit of Measure	Creature's Height/Length	Length of a pencil
mouse	tails	2 tails	3 tails
ant			
elephant			
dwarf			
whale			
giant			
turtle			
goldfish			

Extension: Write a story about one of these creatures. Include your unit of measure in your story when you give details to your readers. For example, "The town of Leighton was 200 tails from Mouse Beri's home."

Social Studies and Science Activities

This chapter provides ways to use students' social studies and science texts for activities as well as offering independent activities related to these disciplines. Creative response, writing, acting, and experimenting are also blended into the ideas in this chapter.

Time Line (social studies or science)

Give each student a piece of construction paper. Instruct them to make an illustrated time line of the period they are studying in social studies or science. To calibrate the time line correctly, students need to use a ruler. Discuss with the class what it means to calibrate (measure in a set unit) before they begin. The time line should be drafted in pencil and checked before color is added. Depending on the amount of time available, you may wish to require five to ten events on the time lines.

1800	1825	1850	1861-1864	1869	1875	1900
			Civil War	Union-Pacific Railroad Completed		

Vocabul"art" (social studies or science)

Either the teacher or the student chooses ten vocabulary words from the social studies or science lesson currently being studied. Direct students to cut two pieces of 9" x 12" construction paper (any colors they like) into quarters to make a book. Staple the pages together or punch holes and tie with string. They should write the title "Vocabulart" on the cover of their book and illustrate it. Each page of the book will contain the vocabulary word, the definition, and a picture illustrating the word's meaning. Students may use their texts and other resources to obtain definitions and ideas for illustrations.

Taste or Smell (science)

Bring several plastic bags of cut up apples, onions, and pears. Also provide several blindfolds and a box of toothpicks. Do not allow students to see the food. Ask students to write down on a piece of paper whether they think smell or taste plays a more important role in identifying food. Collect the votes and count them. Post the results on the board. Next, explain that you are going to do a little experiment to see whether taste or smell actually is more significant. Divide students into groups of three. One student will be the taster, one will be the recorder, and one will be the person who places the food on the tongue of the taster.

Blindfold the tasters and tell them to pinch their noses closed with their fingers. Then ask one student from each group to take a piece of apple, onion, and pear respectively on a toothpick and place it on the taster's tongue. After each item is thoroughly chewed, ask the student who tasted it to identify it. The recorder for each group will keep track of these responses. Students will discover that telling foods apart without the sense of smell is difficult. Following this experiment, read to them from an encyclopedia about the sense of smell to give them some additional information.

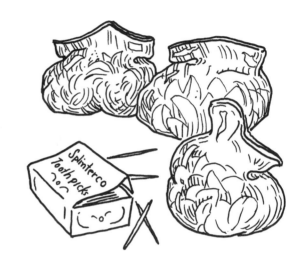

Fingerprints (science)

This activity requires some type of paint and white paper. Fingerpaint would be ideal, but most any paint will work. Distribute a sheet of paper to each student and place desks in table arrangements so that paint can be shared. Show students how to dip their fingers into the paint and make a fingerprint. It will be important that not too much paint is on the finger, or the print will not come out. Have them print all ten fingers and examine each print closely to observe the differences among them. As an extension, students can create a "Wanted" poster with a description of themselves and use their fingerprints as a border.

Emergency Take-Off (science)

Explain to students that the earth is about to be hit by an asteroid and that they have to leave immediately for the moon. They can only take items in their possession or items from the classroom. There is a limit of three items per student (other than clothes). Divide students into groups of four and give the groups five to ten minutes to decide what they are going to take with them. Groups then have a choice of explaining their choices in a story about their "moonlighting" adventure or showing why they think they will need these items through an impromptu skit.

Museum Card (social studies)

Bring in some "artifacts"—objects of some kind which could be construed as artifacts. Tell students that these are objects of a culture that existed either a long time ago or at some point in the future. Place students in groups of three or four and give each group an "artifact." The group's job is to decide what the object was used for, give it a name, and write a museum card for it (see page 44 for the museum card master). Ask groups to read their cards to the rest of the class once all groups have finished. Place the objects and their museum cards on display in the room.

Bird's Eye View (social studies)

Before beginning this activity, talk with students about point of view, or perspective. Help them to understand that where you stand (literally or metaphorically) influences how you see things. Then distribute the student sheet on page 45. Discuss the "bird's eye view" map shown on the page and make certain that they understand the perspective. To emphasize perspective, you may want them also to draw how they see the room from their seats and then contrast the two views.

Map Quiz (social studies)

For this activity, found on page 46, it is a good idea to have a large U.S. map available. This is often hanging at the top of the chalkboard. Students also may have a map in their textbooks. The questions on this quiz refer to all 50 states, so make certain that the maps used include Alaska and Hawaii.

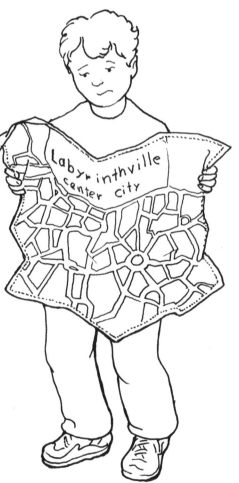

Map of the Stars (social studies)

Prior to beginning this activity, locate a street map in the student text or bring a map of your city that can be xeroxed for students. Spend some time studying the map's features, including those listed on the student handout on page 47. Instruct students to draw the map in pencil first and add color later.

Breathing Rate (science)

Organize students into pairs. Each student will take a turn as the timer and as the subject. Use the recording sheet on page 48 for students to keep track of their data. If the class clock does not have a second hand, you will need a watch that does. Pairs can work independently if the class clock has a second hand or if they have a watch with a second hand. If this is not the case, you will need to be the timer and have the class work as a unit while you watch the time. First, each student needs to count how many normal breaths he or she takes while at rest. Whoever is timing will allow one minute while each student counts his/her breaths. Record this number and repeat for one more minute to check for accuracy. Next, ask students to run in place for two minutes. After this exercise, they need to record the number of breaths they take per minute as they did while at rest. Then ask them to guess what their breathing rate would be while sleeping and to write why they think this.

MUSEUM CARD

ITEM:_____

DESCRIPTION:_____

_____

_____

PROBABLE FUNCTION:_____

_____

_____

_____

MUSEUM CARD

ITEM:_____

DESCRIPTION:_____

_____

_____

PROBABLE FUNCTION:_____

_____

_____

_____

Bird's Eye View

Have you ever flown in an airplane and looked down on the world? If you have, explain how things looked below. If you have not been up in a plane, ask someone who has to describe to you what it looked like.

From an airplane, the world looks _____

_____

_____

_____

_____

_____

_____

Below is a map of a room from a "bird's eye view." Study it and then draw a map of your room from a "bird's eye view." Label everything in the room clearly.

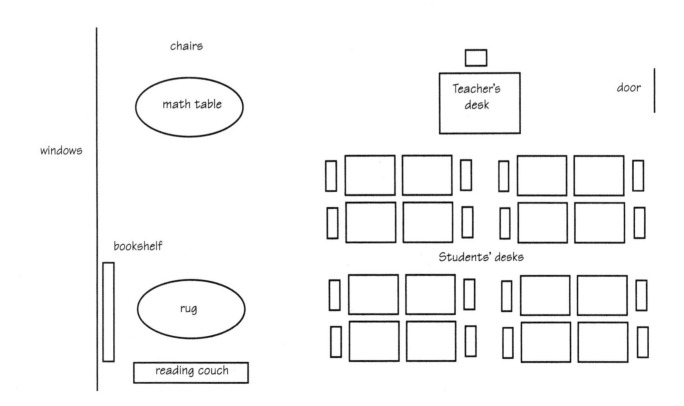

Name _____

Map Quiz

Use a map of the United States to answer the questions below.

1. How many states start with the letter "M"? _____

2. How many states touch one of the Great Lakes or an ocean? _____

3. How many states touch the Canadian border? _____

4. How many states touch the Mexican border? _____

5. How many states do NOT touch any other states? _____

6. How many states are islands? _____

7. How many states are roughly shaped like rectangles? _____

8. How many states touch the Pacific Ocean? _____

9. How many states end with a vowel? _____

10. How many states touch the Atlantic Ocean? _____

Write five questions of your own that can be answered from the U.S. map. Exchange papers with a classmate and try to answer each other's questions. Make certain that you have found the answers to all the questions you write.

_____
_____
_____
_____
_____
_____
_____
_____
_____
_____
_____
_____

Map of the Stars

Choose at least five of your favorite TV, movie, sports, or music stars and create a fictitious map of a "Hollywood" community which shows where each star lives. In addition to the stars' homes, your map should include the following:

a compass rose   a legend   at least four streets and street names

a park   a store   a gas station

You may add anything else you would like to put in your community. To get a better idea of how to draw a street map, use your social studies textbook or an atlas.

Once you have finished your map, write ten questions which can be answered by looking at your map. Include some questions which require the use of north, south, east, or west in order to be answered. For example, "if I were visiting Brad Pitt and he sent me out to the store for some chips, in which direction(s) would I need to travel?" You may write your questions on the lines below. Write an answer key for your questions also.

_____

_____

_____

_____

_____

_____

_____

_____

_____

_____

_____

_____

_____

_____

_____

Breathing Rate

Student Name _____

Normal breathing rate: _____ breaths per minute

Breathing rate after exercise: _____ breaths per minute

Why do you think the breathing rate changed after your exercise? _____
_____

Make a guess about what your breathing rate might be while you are sleeping.
_____ breaths per minute

Why do you make this guess? _____
_____
_____

Breathing Rate

Student Name _____

Normal breathing rate: _____ breaths per minute

Breathing rate after exercise: _____ breaths per minute

Why do you think the breathing rate changed after your exercise? _____
_____

Make a guess about what your breathing rate might be while you are sleeping.
_____ breaths per minute

Why do you make this guess? _____
_____
_____

Presenting activities that focus on the student is a great way to capture student interest and involvement. The ideas in this chapter draw on students' backgrounds and knowledge of themselves and thus provide a great way to "break the ice" as a substitute teacher. In addition, you will gain some insight about the students, and they may find out something useful about themselves and their peers as well.

Student Time Line

Explain to students that they are going to create a time line of their own personal history. To illustrate this for them, draw a time line of your history on the board, highlighting ten major points in your life. Make certain that they understand how to calibrate the time line. Then pass out a large piece (18" x 12") of construction paper and a ruler to each student. It is a good idea for students to draft their time lines in pencil and then go over them with markers. Each student needs to have five to ten significant events on the time line. They can then illustrate some of them and share their finished products with the class.

Student Collage

For this activity, it is a good idea to collect some magazines beforehand and take them to class with you. Direct students to make collages that tell about themselves. They can use pictures and words but should not put their names on the collage. Once they have finished, collect the collages and pass them out randomly so that each student has a collage that is not his or her own. Students will then write a paragraph about the person based on the collage. Ask each student to read the paragraph aloud and then make a guess about whose collage he/she has. It would be helpful to students if you prepare a collage and a paragraph about yourself (based on the collage) to show students before they begin. When the activity is completed, post the collages with their paragraphs around the room. As a follow-up, ask each student to name one new thing they learned about a classmate from this activity.

Say It Symbolically

Prepare a sample of this activity based on yourself. Choose a symbol for yourself, draw and color it, and write the paragraph underneath the picture explaining why it is a good symbol for you. Distribute the student handout on page 51. Read the first two paragraphs aloud to students and then share your symbol with the class. Following this, students can create their own symbols and paragraphs which can be shared with the class and hung about the room.

Goal Ladders

Distribute the student handout on page 52. Read the first paragraph aloud. Then illustrate the activity by writing one short-term and one long-term goal you have for yourself on the board. (You may wish to prepare this in advance and copy it onto the board.) Fill in the rungs of each of your goal ladders with the steps it will take to reach your goal. Begin at the bottom and work up. Then read the second paragraph of the handout to the class and ask students to fill in their own goal ladders. Once completed, students may wish to share their goals with the class.

Getting a job
Going to college
Saving money

Personal Time

Before explaining this activity to students, prepare a sample based on your own habits. Pass out the student handout on page 53 and work through the steps with your example on the board. If possible, use colored chalk to make the pie graph and ask students to use a different color for each activity they include in their pie graph as well. The use of calculators is strongly recommended.

Family Ties

Sharing this activity with the class will help to "break the ice" because you will be offering students some information about yourself. Distribute the student handout on page 54, and then read your family tree and the answers you wrote to the questions to the class. Then direct students to complete the handout. Ask for volunteers who wish to share their responses with the class.

Say It Symbolically

A symbol is anything that stands for or represents something else. For example, the American flag stands for freedom and a white dove means peace.

Symbols are a way of taking an abstract idea and making it more concrete. In the popular movie *Forrest Gump*, a floating feather was used to symbolize the idea that people float about in life, without too much control over what happens to them. Another example of a symbol can be found in John Christopher's book, *The White Mountains*. In this story of life in the future, 13-year-olds are "capped." Being "capped" stands for the loss of a person's ability to think on their own, or a loss of freedom.

Choose a symbol that best describes you. On a separate sheet of paper, draw a picture of it. List below the reasons this is a good symbol for you. Then write a paragraph underneath your picture explaining why you chose this symbol.

Reasons this is a good symbol for me:

_____
_____
_____
_____
_____
_____
_____
_____

Goal Ladders

Goals are what we hope to achieve in our lives. Most of us set short-term goals and long-term goals. Short-term goals are the things we want to see happen soon. These would include something we are striving for today, or next week, or next month. Long-term goals are things we want to see happen in the more distant future, such as next year or five years from now. We have to take steps in order to reach our goals. These steps are the small things that lead us toward our goals.

Think of one short-term and one long-term goal you have for yourself. Some ideas are improving your grade in a certain subject, making the basketball team, going to college, getting a job, making a new friend, or saving your money for a stereo. Write your goal on the top rung of the ladder below. Then fill in the steps you need to take to reach your goal.

Short-Term Goal   **Long-Term Goal**

Personal Time

How do you spend your time? Think about your typical weekday (one 24-hour period) and fill in the chart below. Then follow the steps to convert the hours into percents. Finally, make a pie graph, using a different color for each activity, which shows how much time you spend doing each activity.

Activity	Hours Per Day	Activity	Hours Per Day
Sleeping	_____	Playing	_____
Eating	_____	Watching TV	_____
Going to School	_____	Doing Chores	_____
Doing Homework	_____	Other _____	_____

To convert the hours to percents, do the following:

1. Write the number of hours you spend doing an activity as the numerator of a fraction and 24 (the total hours in a day) as the denominator of the fraction.
   Example: If I spend 6 hours a day sleeping, I would write $\frac{6}{24}$.

2. Using a calculator, enter the numerator and divide it by the denominator.
   Example: $6 \div 24 = .25$ This will give you a decimal answer.

3. Next, multiply the decimal answer by 100 to get a percent.
   Example: $.25 \times 100 = 25\%$.

4. Use the percents to make a pie graph below which shows the approximate time you spend doing various activities. Write the activity and the percent in each area of the pie graph as shown in the example.

Example:

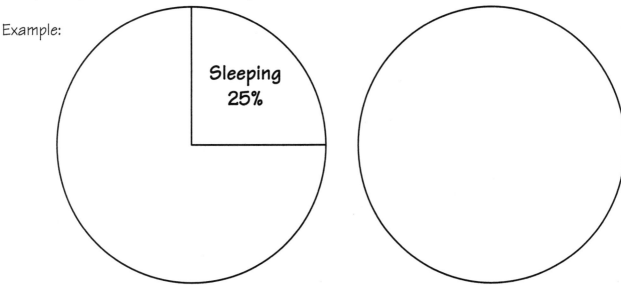

Sleeping
25%

Family Ties

Fill in the family tree below and then answer the questions about your family. If your family is small, you may not need all the lines provided. Feel free to add more lines if necessary.

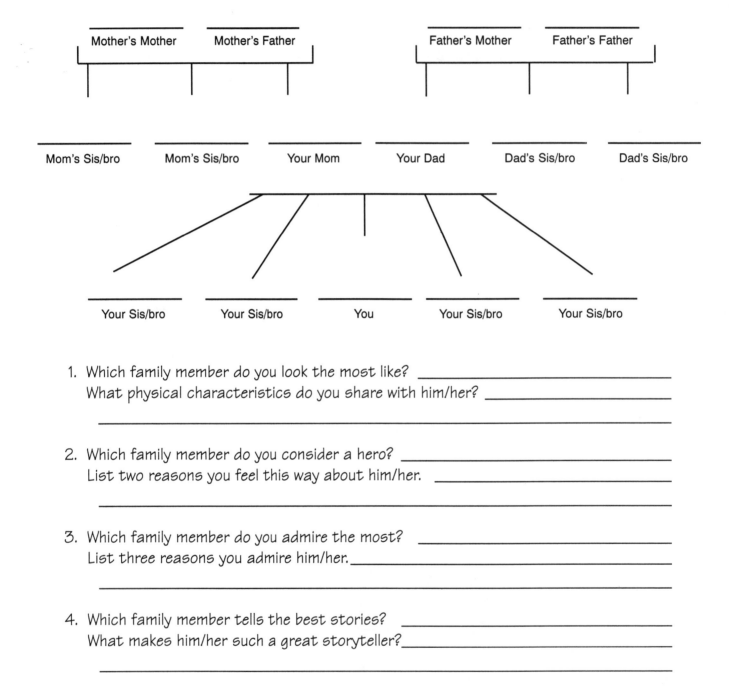

Mother's Mother   Mother's Father   Father's Mother   Father's Father

Mom's Sis/bro   Mom's Sis/bro   Your Mom   Your Dad   Dad's Sis/bro   Dad's Sis/bro

Your Sis/bro   Your Sis/bro   You   Your Sis/bro   Your Sis/bro

1. Which family member do you look the most like? _____
   What physical characteristics do you share with him/her? _____
   _____

2. Which family member do you consider a hero? _____
   List two reasons you feel this way about him/her. _____
   _____

3. Which family member do you admire the most? _____
   List three reasons you admire him/her._____
   _____

4. Which family member tells the best stories? _____
   What makes him/her such a great storyteller?_____
   _____

5. Which family member do you hope to be like when you get older?_____
   List three reasons you want to be like him/her. _____
   _____

CHAPTER 6 Picture Files

Maintaining a picture file that is always ready to go to the job with you can be a blessing. There are many activities that can be generated by such a file. As you assemble your file, include photographs, magazine pictures, old calendar pictures, newspaper pictures, and drawings or photos of artwork.

Captions

On the back of some of your pictures, write statements such as these: "This place is an early childhood memory," "You will live here someday," "This is your favorite food," "You are terrified of this animal," etc. Pass the pictures out randomly to students. Then direct them to turn the pictures over and read the sentence on the back. Ask them to write a detailed description of the picture beginning with that sentence. (They will need to change any "you" statements to "I" statements in order to begin.) Emphasize word choice and attention to detail. You might prepare a sample in advance to illustrate what you would like them to do. When the class has finished writing, collect pictures and descriptions. Line the pictures up on the chalkboard tray or tape them to the chalkboard. Then pass out the descriptions to students who did not write them. Ask each student to read the description and then try to guess which picture goes with it.

Guide to Reproducibles

Haiku and Diamante

Teach the haiku and diamante formats found on pages 57 and 58. Then direct students to choose a picture of a nature setting (if writing a haiku) or a picture of something which conjures up a strong opposite for them (if writing a diamante). If you have the time and the pictures, each student may choose two pictures and write each type of poem. When finished, students can share their pictures and poems with their classmates.

In the News

Bring in a picture from a recent newspaper or magazine (or several pictures if you wish). Tape the picture(s) to the chalkboard and write below them "This /These picture(s) was/were recently in the news. Why?" (see below)

Following this, distribute the student handout on page 59 and direct students to write a news article that goes with one of the pictures. Students may work in pairs if you prefer.

Buy Now!

Collect pictures of items which can be categorized as products (try not to choose those with brand names on them). These pictures will remain with the students, so you will need to replace them after each use. Before beginning the activity, discuss aspects of commercials such as slogans, jingles, color use, music, humor, animals, choice of actors, etc. Ask students to name some products whose commercials come to mind easily. Why do they remember these? Point out that "good" commercials (those that we remember) have some gimmick that sticks in our minds. When you have finished this discussion, divide students into pairs and pass out the student handout on page 60. Each pair needs to choose a picture of a product and then design a commercial for that product. Allow some time (about ten minutes) for pairs to practice their commercial and then ask each pair to perform it for the class.

Color My World?

For this activity, you will need one picture that is in color and one that is in black and white for each group of students. Divide students into small groups of three to four and pass out one color and one black-and-white picture to each group. Direct the groups to focus on the differences between the pictures that are due to the presence or absence of color. Then ask them to complete the student handout on page 61.

Haiku

Haiku is a form of poetry that comes from Japan. It has a strict style that relies on the number of syllables in each line of the poem. The subjects of haikus usually have to do with some aspect of nature and contain only a single thought about a special moment. To begin your haiku, list adjectives and actions about your subject, as well as how the subject makes you feel. For example, if I were trying to write a haiku about a mouse, I might list adjectives, such as "small," "brown," and "furry;" actions, such as "scurries" or "hides;" and a feeling, such as "I'm amazed at how it manages because it is so small." Then I would use these ideas to create my poem, as in the second example below.

Haiku
a three-line poem of 17 syllables
Line 1: 5 syllables
Line 2: 7 syllables
Line 3: 5 syllables

Examples
The mist settles in
Covering the trees and moss
All the forest sleeps

The little brown mouse
Scurrying across the field
Holding on to life

Choose a picture from the picture file that is a nature scene of some kind. Write two haiku about the picture and choose your best one to share with the class.

Haiku #1

_____
_____
_____

Haiku #2

_____
_____
_____

Diamante

The diamante is a poem that begins with one idea and gradually fades to an opposite idea. It has a strict form which results in a diamond-shaped pattern. The "magic" of the diamante occurs in the fourth line, where the writer must begin the transition to the opposite idea. Word choice in this line is particularly important.

Diamante: a seven-line poem of 16 words

1 word
2 adjectives for word in line 1
3 participles for word in line 1
4 nouns—2 related to word in line 1, 2 related to word in line 7
3 participles for word in line 7
2 adjectives for word in line 7
1 word
(opposite)

A good way to begin your diamante is to choose the two opposite ideas before you begin writing the rest of the poem. As you form your poem, choose precise words. Avoid words such as *good, bad, big,* and *little.* The participles in lines three and five need to be words that end in "ing" or "ed."

Dark
Peaceful, Cozy
Relaxing, Discovering, Understanding
Seawater, Night, Stars, Eyes
Laughing, Joking, Dancing
Alive, Brilliant
Light

Choose a picture which suggests a strong opposite to you and write a diamante below

_____

_____   _____

_____   _____   _____

_____   _____   _____   _____

_____   _____   _____

_____   _____

_____

In the News

Study the picture your teacher has assigned to you. Look for details that might help you answer the questions below as accurately as possible. Then write a newspaper article which goes with this picture.

Who is in the picture? _____

_____

What is the person/thing doing in the picture, or what is going on in the picture?

_____

_____

When did the events take place? _____

_____

Where did the events take place? _____

_____

How did the events take place; what caused them to occur? _____

_____

Why is the person or thing doing whatever it is doing in the picture, or why did the event occur? _____

_____

_____

Headline

_____

_____

_____

_____

_____

_____

_____

Buy Now!

Choose a product from the pictures your teacher has supplied. Paste the picture in the space below. Then work with your partner to create a commercial for your product. Develop a slogan (such as "M and M's melt in your mouth, not in your hand!") or a jingle (such as "Oh, I wish I were an Oscar Meyer wiener . . ."). When you have finished writing the commercial, practice it a few times and then perform it for the class.

Slogan or Jingle

_____
_____
_____
_____
_____
_____
_____
_____

Product

Commercial Dialogue

_____
_____
_____
_____
_____
_____
_____
_____
_____
_____
_____
_____

Color My World?

Study the two pictures you have been given. Then answer the questions below. Be certain to include all the feelings and ideas of everyone in your group.

1. Which picture attracts you more (draws your eyes to it)? _____
   What is it that seems to draw you to it? _____
   _____

2. Describe the colors in the color picture. Are there many colors or only a few? Are they vibrant colors? Dull? Shiny? Why do you think these particular colors were chosen for this picture? _____
   _____
   _____
   _____

3. What feelings do you have when you look at the color picture? (excited, quiet, sad, happy, etc.) _____
   _____

4. Describe the black-and-white picture. Is it only black and white, or are there shades of gray? How many different shades do you see? If the picture contains shades of gray, why do you think it is not just black and white? _____
   _____
   _____
   _____

5. What feelings do you have when you look at the black-and-white picture? (excited, quiet, sad, happy, etc.) _____
   _____

6. In your opinion, would the color picture be more effective (a better picture) in black and white? Why or why not? _____
   _____

7. In your opinion, would the black-and-white picture be more effective (a better picture) in color? Why or why not? _____
   _____

7 Novel Ideas

Teacher-Directed Activities

Reading to students, no matter what their age, can be a great way to begin the morning or afternoon. It is an especially useful technique to resettle students after lunch, a break, or a stimulating activity. The stories used in this chapter are all relatively short, which allows them to be read fairly quickly with time left for discussion and/or activities. In addition, many of them have important ideas to offer and hopefully will enlarge students' vision of the world and themselves.

Scavenger Hunt

Write a list of objects, events, people, etc., from the story on the board. Direct students to listen for the items in this list as you read. You can ask them to draw a picture of each item when they hear its description or to raise their hands when they hear it.

Plot Map

Give students a large piece (18" x 12") of white or light-colored construction paper. Before you begin reading to them, discuss the idea of plot (the major events in a story). Then tell them to fold their paper into eighths or sixteenths (whichever you feel is most appropriate). In each resulting box, they are to draw a major event as you read. They can sketch it with pencil while you are reading and color it after the story is finished. Ask students to share their plot maps with the class and to tell why they chose the events they did.

Book Jacket

For this activity, do not tell students the title of the story or show them the cover of the book. After reading a story to the class, ask them to title the story, create a book jacket (cover) for the story, and write a plot summary (which does not disclose the ending) for the back of the book jacket. Ask students to share their book jackets with the class and explain why they titled the book as they did. You might prepare an example of this activity using a different story than the one you plan to read.

Character History

After you read a story to the class, ask students to choose one of the characters from the story. They are to do two things with this character: (1) draw a picture of him/her/it as he/she/it was described in the story (give as much detail as possible), and (2) write the history of the character BEFORE entering this particular story. You might help them brainstorm questions to consider for the history writing and post these on the board. Some examples might be as follows:

1. When and where was the character born? Describe his/her family in the first five years of his/her life. Also describe the house/farm/town/city in which he/she lived.
2. What important events happened to the character before this story began?
3. What challenges did this character face before he/she entered this story?

Group Summary

After you have read the story to the class, write the first sentence of a summary for the story. Then pass the paper around the room so that each student can add the next sentence of the summary. Once the paper has circulated around the room, read the summary aloud. Discuss the idea of plot and enlist students' help in determining which of the events listed are major plot events.

INVITING JASON

E. L. Konigsburg
From: *Altogether, One at a Time*

Aladdin Books. Macmillan Pub. Co. © 1971   ISBN: 0-689-71290-1

This collection of four stories about various relationships and types of people is very appealing to students. While "Inviting Jason" is the story chosen here, the other three stories—"The Night of the Leonids," "Camp Fat," and "Momma at the Pearly Gates"—are equally excellent. All four deal with important issues which challenge students to examine their preconceptions and those of society as well.

"Inviting Jason" is the story of a ten-year-old boy (Stanley) who is having a birthday party. He does not want to invite Jason, who has dyslexia, basically because he has dyslexia. His mother insists, however, and through the context of the party, facts and attitudes about dyslexia are revealed. In the end, Jason's dyslexic way of seeing the world is shown to have a creative advantage.

After reading the story, discuss dyslexia with the class. Ask them what their understanding of it is after listening to "Inviting Jason." Help students to understand that there are different forms of dyslexia, but all of them present difficulties with reading, writing, and spelling. This is not something dyslexic students can help, nor does it ever go away. However, specialized instruction can help to minimize the problems and teach students ways to compensate. It might help to compare having dyslexia to being color-blind. If a color-blind person sees red as blue, for example, (s)he can be trained to understand that every time (s)he sees red, it is blue, but (s)he can never actually see the color red. Similarly, a dyslexic person who sees a "b" as a "p" can be trained to check the rest of the word for a clue as to whether the letter is actually "b" or "p," but (s)he may still be unable to actually see the letter as it appears to everyone else. Following this discussion, ask students to complete the worksheet found on page 69.

THE ELEPHANT'S CHILD

Rudyard Kipling

From: *Just So Stories*

Penguin Books, Ltd. © 1994   ISBN: 0-14-036702-0

This collection of "Porquoi" stories is a classic. Kipling's humorous and unusual writing style adds to the character of the myths and makes them even more appealing. "The Elephant's Child" is the story chosen here, but there are many others within the collection that are just as instructive and enjoyable. Asking students to create their own "Porquoi" stories is an excellent follow-up activity.

"The Elephant's Child" is the story of a young elephant who is (naturally) curious about something that lies beyond his home. He wants to know what the crocodile eats for dinner. He asks all his relatives, who do not answer him, but spank him for asking instead. Eventually, he strikes out on his own to discover what the crocodile eats for dinner. He finds the reptile, who tricks him into coming close to the bank of the river and then grabs his nose. The elephant's child narrowly escapes becoming the crocodile's dinner with the help of his friend the python. However, he discovers that his nose (which was a "mere, smear nose") is now a long trunk. On his way home, he finds many uses for this new nose and when he arrives in his village, he promptly uses his trunk to spank all the relatives that so happily spanked him.

This story could obviously be renamed "How the Elephant Got Its Trunk" and is meant to explain exactly that. Students will enjoy acting out the tale as you read it. Assign parts before beginning. You may wish to switch actors in the middle of the story, perhaps as the elephant's child sets out on his journey.

After reading the story with the class, discuss some of the writing elements used by Kipling in "The Elephant's Child." These include rhyming descriptions (mere, smear nose), repetition of words and phrases ('satiable curtiosity, great green banks of the Limpopo River), and the full circle return to spanking "with a twist."

Next, distribute the student handout on page 70 and direct students to write their own myth and illustrate it. When they are finished, ask them to read it to the class. (You may offer to read it if they do not want to read—this can avoid embarrassment for students who do not read well.) If possible, post the myths and illustrations around the room.

THE MISSING PIECE

Shel Silverstein

Harper & Row Pub. © 1976   ISBN: 0-06-025671-0

This simple story of a "circle" that is missing a piece has a powerful message for everyone about finding happiness or contentment within yourself. It also suggests that the journey of life is what keeps us going, rather than the attainment of our vision of perfection. As the "circle" rolls on throughout the story, it tries piece after piece in its open space but finds problems with all of them. Finally, it ends up realizing that it is happiest without a "piece" and continues on its journey.

While reading this story, be certain to show all the pictures to the class because they communicate much of the story. Once you have finished, ask students to think for a few minutes about the message of the story. Give them about two minutes of silence to do this and then pass out the handout on page 71. Ask them not to discuss the story with their neighbors because you want to know what their personal ideas are. When students are finished with the activity sheet, ask for volunteers to share some of their answers. If you have time, you might ask pairs of students to write and illustrate a sequel to *The Missing Piece*.

THE SECRET LIFE OF WALTER MITTY

James Thurber

From: *Traditions in Literature*

Helen McDonnell. et. al. Scott, Foresman and Co.   © 1991 ISBN: 0-673-29380-7

A well-known tale of the flight of a man into the fantasy of his mind, "The Secret Life of Walter Mitty" is a humorous, yet sad account of a man's need to escape his boring life. Dominated by his nagging wife, Walter Mitty steps into his imagination at every possible moment. He daydreams that he is an expert pilot, a famous doctor, a sharpshooter, and a captured officer who faces the firing squad with pride. There is also a 1947 film version of the story, which might be used as an alternative or follow-up to reading. After reading the story or showing the film, ask students to complete the handout on page 72.

THANK YOU, M'AM

Langston Hughes

A DIP IN THE POOLE

Bill Pronzini

From: *Twists*

Burton Goodman Contemporary Pub. Co. © 1989   ISBN: 0-89061-502-1

Twists contains short stories by many famous authors. All of the stories have a surprise, or unexpected ending, and are very short, which makes them easy to use with students. Two other such books exist in the series, *More Twists* and *Sudden Twists*. You will find these collections well worth having if you substitute for middle school students frequently. "Thank You, M'am" (Langston Hughes) and "A Dip in the Poole" (Bill Pronzini) are the stories chosen here, but you will likely find many other enjoyable tales within these pages to read to your students. Because these stories are very short (two or three pages), you may wish to copy them for students to use as a reference while they complete the handouts.

"Thank You, M'am" is the story of a young, African American boy who tries to steal an older woman's purse. She catches him, however, takes him home, and feeds him. Overall, she treats him very kindly. Her behavior has a profound effect on the child for the rest of his life.

When reading this story, do not show any illustrations to students that would give them clues as to the ethnic origin of the characters. After you have finished reading, divide students into groups of about four and give them the student handout on page 73 to discuss in their group. One person from each group should record the feelings and answers of the group members. Allow about 20 minutes for group discussion and then ask each group to share its members' responses.

"A Dip in the Poole" is a tale of a female pickpocket who is caught in the act of stealing. The twist is that, at first, the reader believes that the woman has been caught by the chief of security for the hotel, but she has actually been "arrested" by another pickpocket, who skillfully weasels away her loot for himself. You will find follow-up questions for this story on the student handout on page 74.

THE MONKEY'S PAW

W. W. Jacobs

From: *Traditions in Literature*

Helen McDonnell. et. al. Scott, Foresman and Co. © 1991   ISBN: 0-673-29380-7

"The Monkey's Paw" is a famous short story which raises a question about fate. In the tale a soldier leaves a "magic" monkey's paw with an old man and his wife. The paw has had a curse placed upon it by a holy man who ". . . wanted to show that fate ruled people's lives, and that those who interfered with it did so to their sorrow." The soldier tells the couple to destroy the paw and warns them that, if they wish upon it, there will be consequences. Curiosity, of course, gets the best of them, and the couple begins a series of three wishes. Dire consequences result and they learn their lesson too late. Or do they? That is the question: would the events that happened to the couple have happened even without the intervention of the monkey's paw? If you believe in fate, or destiny, you must answer yes.

As you read this story to the class, stop at the points below and ask students to write down their predictions. You might have some students share their thoughts before you move on.

1. Pause after the strange man comes to call on the Whites. This sentence ends with ". . . but he was at first strangely silent." Ask students to write down why they think this man has come to the Whites and what he will say.

2. Pause after Mr. White wishes his son alive again. This sentence ends with "'I wish my son alive again.'" Ask students to write down what they think will happen next.

3. Pause after Mr. White admonishes his wife not to open the door. This sentence ends with "'For heaven's sake don't let it in,' cried the old man, trembling." Ask students to write down what they think is knocking at the door.

4. Pause after Mr. White makes his third wish. This sentence ends with ". . . found the monkey's paw and frantically breathed his third and last wish." Ask students what they think he wished. Then ask them to write the last paragraph of the story.

Ask for volunteers to share their endings. Following this, read the actual ending of the story. Then lead a discussion about whether the Whites' loss of their son was due to fate (would have happened anyway) or the monkey's paw. Ask students to explain their thinking. Then ask them to respond in writing to this question: If you had the chance to wish on the monkey's paw, would you do it? Why or why not?

Inviting Jason

"Inviting Jason" is the story of a ten-year-old boy who is having a birthday party. He does not want to invite Jason, who has dyslexia, basically **because** he has dyslexia. His mother insists, however, and through the context of the party, facts and attitudes about dyslexia are revealed. In the end, Jason's dyslexic way of seeing the world is shown to have an advantage.

1. Have you ever known someone who had a learning challenge like Jason? What was your first impression of this person? _____

   _____

   Once you knew this person for a while, did your first impression change? If so, how did it change? _____

2. Do you have a learning challenge? If so, describe what it is like for you in school.

   _____

   _____

3. Imagine for a moment that you and Jason have switched places. What would it be like to walk in Jason's shoes? How might you see things? How might you feel? Write a sentence the way you think Jason might write it.

   _____

   _____

   _____

4. People who are different in some way are often made fun of or considered "bad." Can you think of some times this has happened in your experience? Tell about it below.

   _____

   _____

   _____

   _____

5. If you had been Stanley, would you have acted the same way toward Jason or not? Explain your answer. _____

   _____

Myths—The Elephant's Child

Make-believe stories that explain how things came to be are called *myths*. They usually tell about the creation of gods or the elements of nature (such as wind or sun, or how certain animals were made). Most cultures, past and present, have myths that are passed down through the generations to help explain the world. In Rudyard Kipling's story, "The Elephant's Child," the origin of the elephant's trunk is explained. Write your own myth about the origin of some aspect of nature. Some possibilities are listed below. When you are finished, draw a colorful picture to illustrate your myth and share your work with the class.

- How lightning came to be
- How the earth was formed
- How the sun was made
- Why rabbits live in holes

- Why the zebra has stripes
- How the Appaloosa got its spots
- Why the moon comes out at night
- Why the donkey is stubborn

_____

_____
_____
_____
_____
_____
_____
_____
_____
_____
_____
_____
_____
_____
_____
_____

The Missing Piece

The Missing Piece is about a circle who is missing part of its shape. It travels through the book trying many different shapes. There is always a reason that it does not feel that the shapes work for it. In the end, it still has a missing piece and is singing happily as it goes on its way.

1. Why do you think the circle thought it was necessary to find its missing piece?

   _____

   _____

2. What were some of the reasons the pieces the circle found did not work out? List as many as you can remember. _____

   _____

   _____

   _____

3. What happened when the circle finally found the piece that fit? _____

   _____

   _____

4. What do you think the circle realized by the end of the story? _____

   _____

   _____

5. What do you think the author's message was in this story? _____

   _____

   _____

6. The drawings in this book were very simple—lines, circles, and triangles in black and white. Do you think the drawings helped to illustrate the message in the story? Explain your reasons for thinking as you do. _____

   _____

   _____

   _____

7. If you were to write a sequel to *The Missing Piece*, what would you call it? Why would you choose this title? _____

   _____

The Secret Life of Walter Mitty

A well-known tale of the flight of a man into the fantasy of his mind, "The Secret Life of Walter Mitty" is a humorous, yet sad account of a man's need to escape his boring life. Dominated by his nagging wife, Walter Mitty steps into his imagination at every possible moment. He daydreams that he is an expert pilot, a famous doctor, a sharpshooter, and a captured officer who faces the firing squad with pride.

1. Why do you think Walter daydreams so often? _____

   _____

2. What can you tell about Walter from the content of his daydreams? How do the daydreams show you what Walter really thinks of himself? _____

   _____

3. Is the "Walter" in real life similar to or different from the "Walter" in the daydreams? Explain how the two "Walters" are the same/different. _____

   _____

   _____

   _____

4. Do you ever daydream? Do you think daydreams are useful? Explain your answer.

   _____

   _____

   _____

5. If you daydreamed like Walter, what would your daydreams be like? In the space below, write an excerpt from your "secret life."

   _____

   _____

   _____

   _____

   _____

   _____

Thank You, M'am

"Thank You, M'am" is the story of a young, African American boy who tries to steal an older woman's purse. She catches him, however, takes him home, feeds him and, overall, treats him very kindly. Her behavior has a profound effect on the child for the rest of his life.

Discuss the questions below with your group. Choose a recorder to write down your group's responses.

1. What clues in the story lead you to believe that the characters are probably African American? _____

   _____

2. Why do you think Mrs. Luella Bates Washington Jones took Roger home and did so many nice things for him? _____

   _____

3. Why do you think Mrs. Luella Bates Washington Jones gave Roger the money to buy the blue suede shoes? _____

   _____

4. If Roger had tried to steal your purse, what would you have done? Explain why you would have acted in this way. _____

   _____

   _____

   _____

5. Would you have given Roger the money for the shoes? Why or why not?

   _____

   _____

   _____

6. What lesson do you think Mrs. Luella Bates Washington Jones was trying to teach Roger? Do you think she succeeded? Give reasons for your thoughts. _____

   _____

   _____

   _____

A Dip in the Poole

"A Dip in the Poole" describes a tale of a female pickpocket who is caught in the act of stealing. The twist is that, at first, the reader believes that the woman has been caught by the chief of security for the hotel, but she has actually been "arrested" by another pickpocket, who skillfully weasels away her loot for himself.

1. When the man first stopped the woman pickpocket, what did you think he was going to do to her? Were you surprised at what he did do? _____

_____

_____

2. What does the man posing as the "chief of security" promise to do with the items that were stolen? What does he make the woman promise him? _____

_____

_____

3. When did you first get suspicious that the "chief of security" was not who he claimed to be? What made you suspicious? _____

_____

4. Do you think the woman will keep her promise about staying away from the hotel? Why or why not? Why was this promise such a good idea from the man's point of view?

_____

_____

_____

5. Why is the title of this story a "play on words"? What did you think it was going to be about when the teacher first read the title? _____

_____

_____

6. If you had been the woman, what would you have done when the man caught you by the arm? _____

_____

_____

_____

Art

Some of the activities in this chapter require advance assembly of materials. As a substitute, it might be a good idea to keep a bag ready with the supplies for one or more of these projects so that it is easy to take it with you when you get that early-morning call.

Word Chain

Materials:
colored construction paper (9" x 12")
scissors (at least 5 pairs)
staplers (several)
markers
dictionaries (or textbook glossaries)

Procedure:
1. Ask students to cut the construction paper into strips about two inches wide (12 inches long).
2. Direct students to choose 5–10 vocabulary words from a certain novel or text.
3. Students write the word on one side of the strip and its definition on the other.
4. Students make a word chain, interlocking the strips and stapling them together.

This activity can be based around any subject. You may wish to have students choose words from the current novel they are reading or from a textbook such as science or social studies. The word chain offers an interesting way to cover vocabulary and can instantly provide a colorfully decorated room as well.

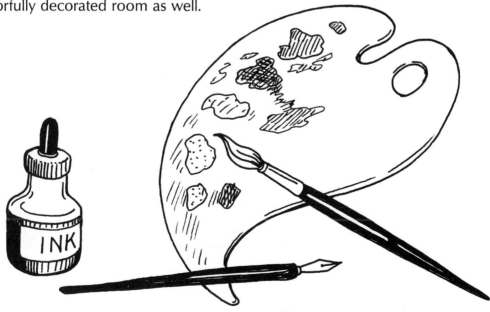

Mobile

Materials:

metal hangers (1 for each student, or 1 for each 2 students)
colored construction paper (9" x 12")
scissors (at least 5 pairs)
a roll of string
single hole punch (several if possible)
markers
dictionaries (or textbook glossaries)

Procedure:

1. Ask students to cut the construction paper into shapes. These could be geometric shapes, such as a triangle, square, etc., or other shapes, such as a person, a dog, etc. Shapes should be fairly large (4" x 6" minimum) so that there is room for drawing on one side and writing on the other.
2. Students will draw pictures on one side and write a description (or sentence) on the other.
3. Students will punch holes in their mobile pieces, cut string of various lengths, and attach their pieces to the hanger to make their mobile.

This activity can be based on many topics. Some suggestions include:

*   Story elements of a book they have read (characters, plot, theme, conflict, resolution, setting)
*   Vocabulary words from any novel or subject they are studying
*   The student's family
*   Important events in the student's personal history
*   Special people in the student's life
*   Places the student has visited

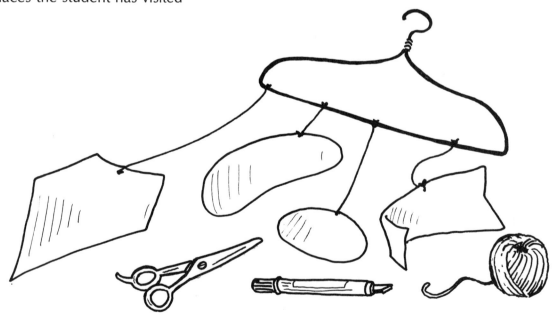

Rock Statues

Materials:
rocks and pebbles of many different sizes, shapes, and colors
sticky tack or crazy glue
markers

Procedure:
1. If the school is located in an area where students can collect their own rocks, take them outside to do so. Otherwise, allow them to choose from the rocks you have brought with you.
2. Explain to students that they will be creating a statue from the rocks. An interesting story to tell here is that of the "Pet Rock," which was just such a creation that became a fad a number of years ago. Believe it or not, people actually paid money for these simple rock statues!
3. Allow students to choose rocks and form them into statues. They may also draw on the rocks to create additional effects.

Crystal Ball

Materials:
food storage bags (not the type that zip closed)
1 package of rubber bands (1 to a student with extras for those that break)
wispy cotton (enough for students to have a good handful each)
construction paper
markers
glue

Procedure:
1. Ask students to think about something they might be doing in 25 years. Calculate with them how old they will be in 25 years.
2. Direct students to draw a picture of themselves in 25 years and cut it out. The resulting figure should be no larger than 5 inches by 5 inches.
3. Pass out one food storage bag, a good-sized handful of wispy cotton, and 1 rubber band to each student.

4. Placing the picture of themselves in the middle of the cotton, students will then need to pull the cotton apart so that it looks like see-through clouds and helps the picture stand upright. It may be necessary to use a little glue to attach the picture to the cotton in several spots.

5. Finally, students need to place the food storage bag around the picture and cotton in a ball-like shape, blow into the bag to create a balloon effect, and place the rubber band on the bottom to hold the "crystal ball" together. The corners of the bag can be tucked in to create a more ball-like crystal ball.

Sculptures

Materials:
poster board
clay, foil, and/or construction paper
tape or sticky tack
scissors

Procedure:
1. Cut the poster board into squares about 6 inches by 6 inches to serve as the base for the statue.
2. Ask students to choose from one of the ideas below and create a sculpture based on that idea (or offer another idea for a sculpture).
3. Demonstrate how the various materials may be used. For example, designs can be cut out of the foil and then the foil can be crinkled up to create a certain effect. Construction paper may be torn instead of cut for a mosaic appearance. Clay, of course, can be molded in many ways and attached to other media if a mixed-media look is desired.
4. When finished, ask students to explain their sculptures to the class.

This activity can be based on many topics. Some suggestions:

- Create a character from a favorite book you have read.
- Create an abstract art sculpture (mixed media is possible here, such as clay, foil, colored paper, etc.)
- Create a statue of someone you consider a hero.
- Create a monument to a special person or to commemorate an important event.

Travel Brochure

Materials:
white construction paper
old magazines
glue sticks
scissors
samples of travel brochures
crayons or markers

Procedure:
1. Give each student a piece of construction paper. Direct them to fold it in thirds.

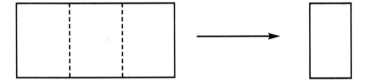

2. After viewing several travel brochures, they can choose a place to advertise and begin creating their own travel brochure. They may use magazine pictures, draw their own pictures, or combine the two. They will also need to write "copy" for the brochure, enticing people to visit.

Medal of Honor

Materials:
foil (silver or gold)
yarn
glue sticks
scissors
construction and/or tissue paper
glitter

Procedure:
1. Explain to students that they are to create a "Medal of Honor" for someone they feel deserves it. Encourage them to be artistic in their medal creation. Medals can be any shape; they do not need to be round.
2. The completed medal should have the following printed on it:

MEDAL OF HONOR
for

_____

Your Dream House

Materials:
graph paper (1 cm squares are preferable)
pencils
rulers

Procedure:

1. Explain to students that they are going to create a blueprint for their dream house. They will need to include the following as they make their plans:

kitchen	bedrooms	bathrooms	hallways
doors	windows	living room	

Optional would be:

study (or den)	family room	garage	laundry room

2. Each square of the graph paper stands for 1 square foot of room. Once the floor plan is drawn, have students write the dimensions of each room inside it. If you like, you can have them go one step further and calculate the area of each room. For example:

```
┌──────────────────────────────────┐
│                                   │
│           Living Room             │
│            24' x 8'               │
│          A = 192 sq feet          │
│                                   │
└──────────────────────────────────┘
```

3. Each part of the plan should be clearly labeled, including widths of doorways and dimensions of hallways and windows.

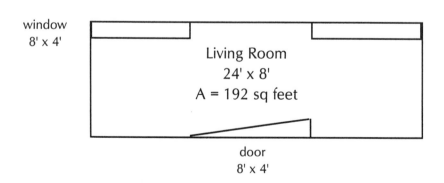

window
8' x 4'

Living Room
24' x 8'
A = 192 sq feet

window
8' x 4'

door
8' x 4'

Torn Paper Picture

Materials:
colored construction paper
glue sticks

Procedure:
1. Explain to students that they are going to create a picture using only torn paper. They can tear actual shapes (such as that of a person) or tear small bits of paper and paste these together to form a more mosaic picture. If you wish, you may give them a topic related to something they are studying, such as: a picture of something that happened during the American Revolution, or a picture of a scientific discovery, or a scene from a novel they are reading, etc.
2. Ask students to share their pictures with the class when they are finished.

Business Card

Materials:
white paper (such as the type used in copy machines)
fine-tipped markers
samples of several different types of business cards

Procedure:
1. Show students the different business cards you have brought with you. Ask them to look for similarities and differences in the cards.
2. After giving them some time to look at the cards, ask students to name the similarities and record them on the board. Discuss what information all business cards usually contain (person's name, person's title, phone number, address, fax number, e-mail address).
3. Next, discuss differences between the cards (such as layout, use of pictures or logos, typefaces, use of color, and other design aspects).
4. Following this discussion, distribute markers and paper to students and instruct them to create their own business cards. It is a good idea to remind them to draft their ideas in pencil. Obviously, these "cards" will not be sized correctly, but it is often true that designs are developed on a larger scale and then reduced to the desired scale. This can be explained to students and, if possible, their designs can be reduced on a xerox machine and distributed to classmates.

Music Montage

Materials:

2 or 3 musical selections that are very different from one another

tapes or CDs

tape or CD player

markers and/or crayons

construction paper

Procedure:

1. Explain to students that you would like them to draw while listening to the music. The drawing can be free form; it does not need to be representational. Be certain to tell them that it is important that no one talks while the music is playing.
2. Distribute markers, crayons, and paper.
3. Play the different types of music. You may either have students stop drawing and begin a new drawing when you change the music or have them continue drawing throughout the change of music.
4. Once the music is finished, ask students to examine their pictures and write about the differences in their drawings. Direct them to focus on color changes, changes in pressure, or type of stroke (such as zigzag or lines, versus circles).
5. Following this activity, ask students to share with their classmates what they have learned about how music influences them.

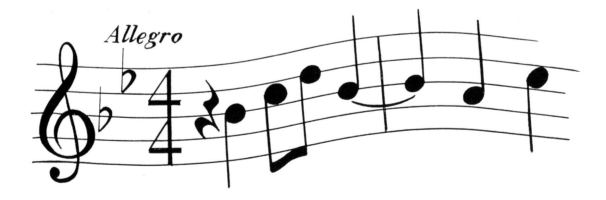

Fictitious Newspaper

Materials:
student handout on page 84
old magazines, scissors (1 for each student)
glue sticks (at least 10)
1 actual newspaper

Procedure:
1. Divide students into groups to cover the usual sections in a newspaper. Include the following categories: front-page news, sports, economy/financial, human interest, and arts/entertainment.
2. Give each group a copy of the section of the newspaper that covers their category and several magazines. Give each student a copy of the handout on page 84.
3. Explain to students that each person in the group is to do the following: a) choose a picture from one of the magazines that relates to their assigned category, and b) write an article to go with that picture.
4. When all the pages are completed, they can be assembled into a class newspaper. Ask students for suggestions for the name of the newspaper and have the class vote to choose it.

Centaurs and More

Materials: student handout on centaurs (found on page 85)
picture of a centaur (if possible)
markers and/or crayons
construction paper

Procedure:
1. Ask if anyone has heard of a centaur. If so, ask them to tell what they know about the creature.
2. Distribute the student handout on page 85.
3. Read the definition and information about the centaur and explain the student activity.
4. Distribute construction paper and markers/crayons for student use in drawing their mythical beast.
5. Allow students to explain their creations and show them to the class when finished.

Section _____ _____

Place headline here

Place picture here

_____   _____
_____   _____
_____   _____
_____   _____
_____   _____
_____   _____
_____   _____
_____   _____
_____   _____
_____   _____
_____   _____
_____   _____
_____   _____
_____   _____
_____   _____
_____   _____
_____   _____

Centaurs and More

The centaur is a creature from Greek mythology who was said to be half man and half horse. According to mythology, the centaurs were the offspring of Ixion (IHK sy uhn) and Nephele (NEHF uh lee). They were men from head to waist and horse from the waist down. Most of them were brutal, but some were wise. Chiron (KY ruhn), who was the wisest centaur, was an expert in music, healing, archery, the care of animals, and prophecy. He taught these arts to many Greek heroes. It is thought that the myth of the centaur originated during the Spanish invasion of the Aztecs. The Aztecs apparently had never seen men mounted on horseback before and thought that the Spaniards could magically divide themselves into men on the ground and half-men (on horseback) whenever they chose.

Invent a creature that is part human and part animal. Decide what physical characteristics your creature will take from each being. Then choose special abilities and personality traits that your creature will "borrow" from the human and the animal. Finally, draw a picture of your mythical beast.

My creature's physical human portion will be _____
Human characteristics (physical traits, abilities, personality traits): _____

_____

_____

_____

_____

My creature's physical animal portion will be _____
Animal characteristics (physical traits, abilities, personality traits): _____

_____

_____

_____

_____

Chapter One
Similes and Metaphors   Page 11
- S 1. Wind is being compared to a small child's breath.
- M 2. She is being compared to a devil.
- S 3. The way the boy walks is being compared to the way a turtle moves.
- M 4. The children's minds are being compared to birds flying free.
- S 5. The girl's spirit is being compared to a soaring bird.

Tips, Please   Page 12

Dollar Amount	10%	15%	20%
$23.00	2.30	3.45	4.60
$65.00	6.50	9.75	13.00
$48.00	4.80	7.20	9.60

"Check" It Out   Page 13
The most money that can be spent without going over the $200.00 would involve the following purchases: tennis racket (82.36), groceries (51.29), skateboard (38.03), pizza (12.37), video game rental (10.15), and ice cream (5.46) for a total of $199.66; with $.34 leftover.

Chapter Two
Songs   Page 17
Rhyme scheme—the pattern of end rhyme in a poem/song. Each ending rhyme is given a letter, beginning with "a" and continuing through the alphabet. Thus the poem below would have the rhyme scheme abab.

I like cats	(a)
I do, you see	(b)
Cats eat rats	(a)
Merci, merci!	(b)

Refrain or *chorus*—the portion of a song that is repeated several times throughout the tune.
Imagery—any words which appeal strongly to one or more of the five senses.
Theme—the main message of the song.

Cryptic Codes   Page 22
CRYPTIC CODES ARE FUN!
DSZQUJD DPEFT BSF GVO!

That's Just Nonsense!   Page 24
Answers will vary depending on word use in the sentences. Sample answers:

- snorber: The snorber was constantly annoying me.
  Part of speech: Noun
- bruzzed: "This is enough!" bruzzed Jake brusquely.
  Part of speech: Verb
- dafolly: She laughed dafolly as she watched the film.
  Part of speech: Adverb
- hiderlada: The hiderlada was motionless, staring me down.
  Part of speech: Noun
- af: The boat was af the harbor.
  Part of speech: Preposition

Chapter Three
On Sale Today   Page 30

Fraction	(Num ÷ Den) =	Decimal	Dec x 100 =	Percent
½	1 ÷ 2 =	.50	.50 x 100 =	50%
²⁵⁄₁₀₀ (¼)	25 ÷ 100 =	.25	.25 x 100 =	25%
⁷⁵⁄₁₀₀ (¾)	75 ÷ 100 =	.75	.75 x 100 =	75%
³⁵⁄₁₀₀	35 ÷ 100 =	.35	.35 x 100 =	35%
⁷⁄₁₀	7 ÷ 10 =	.70	.7 x 100 =	70%

Item	Discount	Original Price	Amt of Discount	Sale Price
Jeans	25% off	$35.00	$8.25	$26.75
T-Shirt	⅓ off	$22.00	$7.26	$14.74
Tennis shoes	50% off	$75.00	$37.50	$37.50
CD Player	¼ off	$150.00	$37.50	$112.50
Skateboard	33% off	$85.00	$28.05	$56.95

Don't Forget the Tax   Page 31

Original Price	Tax Rate	Decimal (Tax Rate ÷ 100)	Amount of Tax (Item Cost x Dec)	Total Price (Orig Price + Tax)
$35.99	5%	5 ÷ 100 = .05	35.99 x .05 = 1.80	35.99 + 1.80 = $37.79
$103.68	10%	10 ÷ 100 = .10	103.68 x .10 = 10.37	103.68 + 10.37 = 114.05
$5.52	4%	4 ÷ 100 = .04	5.52 x .04 = .22	5.52 + .22 = 5.74
$243.25	7%	7 ÷ 100 = .07	243.25 x .07 = 17.03	243.25 + 17.03 = 260.28
$26.75	8%	8 ÷ 100 = .08	26.75 x .08 = 2.14	26.75 + 2.14 = 28.89
$98.31	15%	15 ÷ 100 = .15	98.31 x .15 = 14.75	98.31 + 14.75 = 113.06
$12.44	6%	6 ÷ 100 = .06	12.44 x .06 = .75	12.44 + .75 = 13.19
$7.37	12%	12 ÷ 100 = .12	7.37 x .12 = .88	7.37 + .88 = 8.25
$525.26	6%	6 ÷ 100 = .06	525.26 x .06 = 31.52	525.26 + 31.52 = 556.78

Pizza Party Pages 33-34

1. 8 divisions, 1 piece pepperoni/cheese, 2 pieces black olives/cheese.

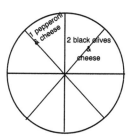

2. 6 divisions, 3 pieces onions/green peppers, 2 pieces pepperoni/black olives.

3. 12 divisions on all 3 pizzas. Pizza one has 6 pieces with pepperoni only and 6 pieces with cheese only. Pizza two has 4 pieces with black olives, 4 pieces with green pepper and onions, and 4 pieces with mushrooms. Pizza three has 5 pieces with everything on them.

Pizza 1   Pizza 2   Pizza 3

4. 16 divisions, 3 pieces pineapple/ham, 4 pieces pepperoni.

Palindromic Fun Page 35

Number	Steps to Palindrome	Palindromic Result
64	2	121
1234	1	5555
122	1	343
3267	4	79497
409	2	4444
78	4	4884

Inches, Feet, or Yards? Page 36

Units most appropriate:

thumb	inches
desktop	inches
chalkboard	feet/yards
pencil	inches
board eraser	inches
book	inches
height of wall	feet/yards
door	feet/yards
your height	feet
paper clip	inches

Chapter Four
Map Quiz Page 46

1. 8 (MI, MN, MO, MS, MT, ME, MA, MD)
2. 30 (MN, WI, IL, MI, IN, OH, PA, NY, ME, NH, MA, RI, CT, NJ, MD, DE, VA, NC, SC, GA, FL, AL, MS, LA, TX, CA, OR, WA, AK, HI)
3. 11 (AK, WA, ID, MT, ND, MN, MI, NY, VT, ME, NH)
4. 4 (CA, AZ, NM, TX)
5. 2 (AK, HI)
6. 1 (HI)
7. 5 (WY, ND, SD, KS, CO)
8. 5 (WA, OR, CA, AK, HI)
9. 32 (HI, AK, CA, NV, ID, MT, CO, AZ, NM, ND, SD, NE, OK, MN, IA, MO, LA, MS, IN, OH, TN, AL, GA, PA, VA, WV, NC, SC, FL, ME, NH, DE)
10. 14 (ME, NH, MA, RI, NY, CT, NJ, MD, DE, VA, NC, SC, GA, FL)

Chapter Seven
The Missing Piece Page 71

Possible answers:

1. It felt incomplete in some way.
2. Pieces were: their "own" piece, too small, too big, too sharp, too square, slipped out, and got crushed.
3. It couldn't do some of the things it liked to do, such as sing.
4. The circle may have realized that it didn't really need a piece to be whole.

5. The author's message may have been that it is the journey of life that makes it interesting, and/or that we have all we need to be whole inside of us and don't need to seek it elsewhere.

The Secret Life of Walter Mitty   Page 72
Possible answers:
1. Walter has a boring life in which his wife dominates and belittles him. He needs to escape it.
2. Walter's daydreams suggest that he does not view himself as a person who is confident or makes a difference. He wishes to be a hero, a "man of substance."
3. The Walter in real life is in direct contrast to the Walter of the daydreams. The former is ineffectual and has a mundane existence. The latter is daring, adventurous, and lives an exciting life.

Thank You, M'am   Page 73
Possible answers:
1. The clues include the dialect and the woman's name, Mrs. Luella Bates Washington Jones.
2. She realized that he had no one to look after him or care for him and she decided to do so.
3. She gave him the money because she was kind and because she wanted him to have the shoes without stealing for them.
6. Mrs. Jones was trying to teach Roger kindness, honesty, and to take a different approach to life. Yes, because it is indicated in the last paragraph that Roger was deeply touched by what she had done for him.

A Dip in the Poole   Page 74
Possible answers:
1. It seems likely that he will arrest her.
2. He promises to return them to the owner. He makes her promise not to ever come back to the Hotel Poole.
3. The first clue comes when the "detective" doesn't turn her in to the police. This is a very odd action (or lack thereof) on his part.
4. She will probably keep her promise since the "detective" would easily recognize her again. This was a clever idea the man had because it left the hotel open for him to pickpocket without competition.
5. The title is a play on words because "A Dip in the Poole" can mean a swim in a pool or a pickpocket in a hotel.